BOSTON HISTORY
for KIDS

 with 21 Activities

FROM RED COATS TO RED SOX

Richard Panchyk

Foreword by Michael Dukakis

CHICAGO REVIEW PRESS

Copyright © 2018 by Richard Panchyk
Foreword © 2018 Michael Dukakis
All rights reserved
Published by Chicago Review Press Incorporated
814 North Franklin Street
Chicago, Illinois 60610
ISBN 978-1-61373-712-5

Library of Congress Cataloging-in-Publication Data
Names: Panchyk, Richard, author.
Title: Boston history for kids : from red coats to Red Sox with 21 activities
   / Richard Panchyk.
Description: Chicago : Chicago Review Press, 2018. | Includes bibliographical
   references and index.
Identifiers: LCCN 2017035960 (print) | LCCN 2017036694 (ebook) | ISBN
   9781613737132 (pdf) | ISBN 9781613737156 (epub) | ISBN 9781613737149
   (kindle) | ISBN 9781613737125 (pbk. : alk. paper)
Subjects: LCSH: Boston (Mass.)—History—Juvenile literature.
Classification: LCC F73.33 (ebook) | LCC F73.33 .P36 2018 (print) | DDC
   974.4/61—dc23
LC record available at https://lccn.loc.gov/2017035960

Cover and interior design: Sarah Olson
Front cover images: Paul Revere statue and Old North Church: Shutterstock/Jorge Salcedo;
1806 Boston map: Wikimedia Commons/Boston Public Library; 1954 Bowman Ted Williams:
Wikimedia Commons/Bowman Gum; Boston Common swan boats: 123rf.com/Antonio Belaguer
Soler; Boston Tea Party, New State House, and Long Wharf: Library of Congress.
Back cover images: Boston Light: Shutterstock/Greg Kushmerek; Boston Freedom Trail sign:
Shutterstock/jiawangkun; Ship model: 123RF Stock Photo/ruzanna; Baseball glove and bat:
Shutterstock/eurobanks
Interior images: Courtesy of the Library of Congress, unless otherwise indicated.
Activity illustrations: Page 61, B. Kulak; page 63, Mark Baziuk; page 113, Jim Spence
Printed in the United States of America
5 4 3 2 1

CONTENTS

FOREWORD

WHEN I WAS YOUNG, I loved Boston, and I loved its history.

One of my favorite books was *Johnny Tremain* by Esther Forbes. It was the story of a young apprentice silversmith who worked for Paul Revere and was deeply involved in the events in Boston that led to the Revolutionary War and America's independence.

It was fictional, but it was set in the colonial Boston of the time and for me was about as realistic as you could get. It told about the early efforts and battles in and around Boston that began our war of independence, and because Revere's home and silversmith shop were in the North End of Boston, I used to take the book under my arm and walk around that part of the city imagining that I might be Johnny and thinking about what it must have been like for a teenager in his position as he observed and participated in the momentous events that led to the Declaration of Independence and our successful war to end British rule and create a new democracy here in the New World.

Unfortunately, Bostonians at the time didn't treasure their history as much as they should have. Boston was dirty. Boston Harbor, one of the world's great natural harbors, was badly polluted, and one of our harbor islands was the site of a glue factory. Many of the city's historic buildings had been torn down for parking lots.

An ugly elevated highway known as the Central Artery was built right through some of Boston's most historic places, just a stone's throw from Revere's home. And we were told that if we were going to solve the city's growing traffic problems, we would have to build a new highway system that would have permanently destroyed historic neighborhoods and a world-renowned park system called the Emerald Necklace.

Finally, in the late 1960s, people here in Boston and Massachusetts and communities all over the country began to understand what we were doing to our historic communities and the legacy their histories had left to us. After 10 years of debate, we finally killed the so-called Master Highway Plan and began investing in a first rate transit system that preserved and didn't destroy so much that makes Boston priceless.

Boston Harbor was cleaned up; its islands restored; and a wonderful national and state harbor islands park system created that should be a must on your vacation or weekend schedule. The city's docks, which played such a role in our history, were uncovered and restored, and today thousands of our citizens and our visitors from all over the world walk, dine, and enjoy our waterfront. That process continues as we work to protect, preserve, and restore the heritage that we inherited from immigrants from all over the world like my parents who came to Boston, made it their home, and helped to create the lovely city that we live in and enjoy today.

Of course, that means that we also have a solemn obligation to continue to preserve and treasure it. Every once in a while, some well-intentioned person or developer will come along with plans for development that could have a profound effect on what Boston means and what it teaches us about the hard job of building and maintaining a genuine and expanding democracy that works for everyone.

Enjoy the most walkable city in America. Study its history carefully. Be inspired, as I was, to try to make a real contribution to it and its future. And walk its streets and alleys and waterfront, as I did, imagining what it was like back in those colonial days and thinking about what you can do to make it even better.

Michael Dukakis
Massachusetts governor, 1975–1979, 1983–1991

TIME LINE

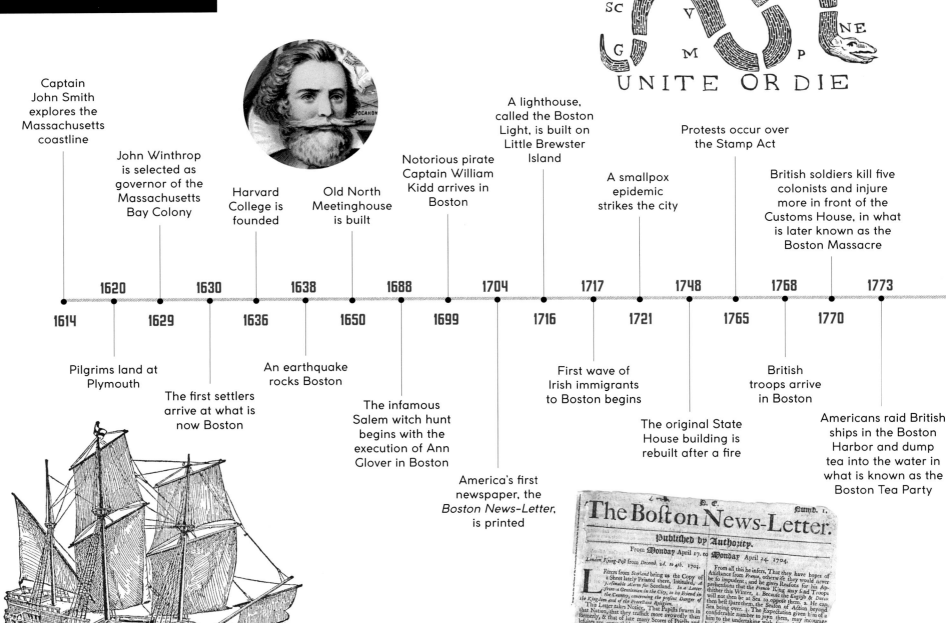

UNITE OR DIE

Captain John Smith explores the Massachusetts coastline

John Winthrop is selected as governor of the Massachusetts Bay Colony

Harvard College is founded

Old North Meetinghouse is built

Notorious pirate Captain William Kidd arrives in Boston

A lighthouse, called the Boston Light, is built on Little Brewster Island

A smallpox epidemic strikes the city

Protests occur over the Stamp Act

British soldiers kill five colonists and injure more in front of the Customs House, in what is later known as the Boston Massacre

1620   **1630**   **1638**   **1688**   **1704**   **1717**   **1748**   **1768**   **1773**

1614   **1629**   **1636**   **1650**   **1699**   **1716**   **1721**   **1765**   **1770**

Pilgrims land at Plymouth

The first settlers arrive at what is now Boston

An earthquake rocks Boston

The infamous Salem witch hunt begins with the execution of Ann Glover in Boston

First wave of Irish immigrants to Boston begins

The original State House building is rebuilt after a fire

British troops arrive in Boston

Americans raid British ships in the Boston Harbor and dump tea into the water in what is known as the Boston Tea Party

America's first newspaper, the *Boston News-Letter*, is printed

The Boston News-Letter.

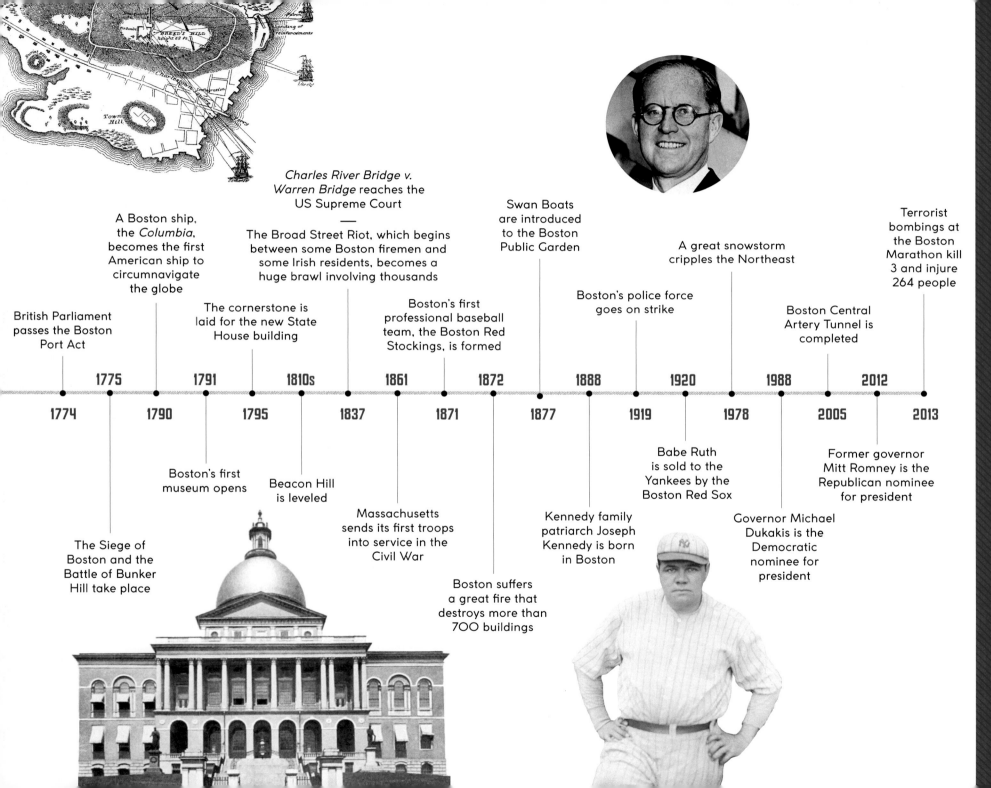

Charles River Bridge v. Warren Bridge reaches the US Supreme Court
—
The Broad Street Riot, which begins between some Boston firemen and some Irish residents, becomes a huge brawl involving thousands

A Boston ship, the *Columbia*, becomes the first American ship to circumnavigate the globe

Swan Boats are introduced to the Boston Public Garden

Terrorist bombings at the Boston Marathon kill 3 and injure 264 people

A great snowstorm cripples the Northeast

British Parliament passes the Boston Port Act

The cornerstone is laid for the new State House building

Boston's first professional baseball team, the Boston Red Stockings, is formed

Boston's police force goes on strike

Boston Central Artery Tunnel is completed

1775 **1791** **1810s** **1861** **1872** **1888** **1920** **1988** **2012**

1774 1790 1795 1837 1871 1877 1919 1978 2005 2013

Boston's first museum opens

Beacon Hill is leveled

Babe Ruth is sold to the Yankees by the Boston Red Sox

Former governor Mitt Romney is the Republican nominee for president

The Siege of Boston and the Battle of Bunker Hill take place

Massachusetts sends its first troops into service in the Civil War

Kennedy family patriarch Joseph Kennedy is born in Boston

Governor Michael Dukakis is the Democratic nominee for president

Boston suffers a great fire that destroys more than 700 buildings

INTRODUCTION

BOSTON IS A VERY SPECIAL and unique place. Not only is it steeped in America's colonial history, from the Puritans who founded the city to the patriotic heroes of the Revolutionary era, but it is also a truly modern metropolis. That mix of old and new makes Boston both a great place to visit and a fascinating and important place to learn about.

This book spans 400 years of Boston history, covering some of the major events that have occurred there, from earthquakes to witch hunts, from the Tea Party to the Great Fire. As you read, you'll meet some of the colorful characters who have walked its streets, and have the chance to do some interesting Boston-related activities along the way.

Having lived in Massachusetts for three years, it was especially fun and exciting for me to write this book, and I sincerely hope that you will enjoy reading it and will use it as the start of further exploration of the city and its history.

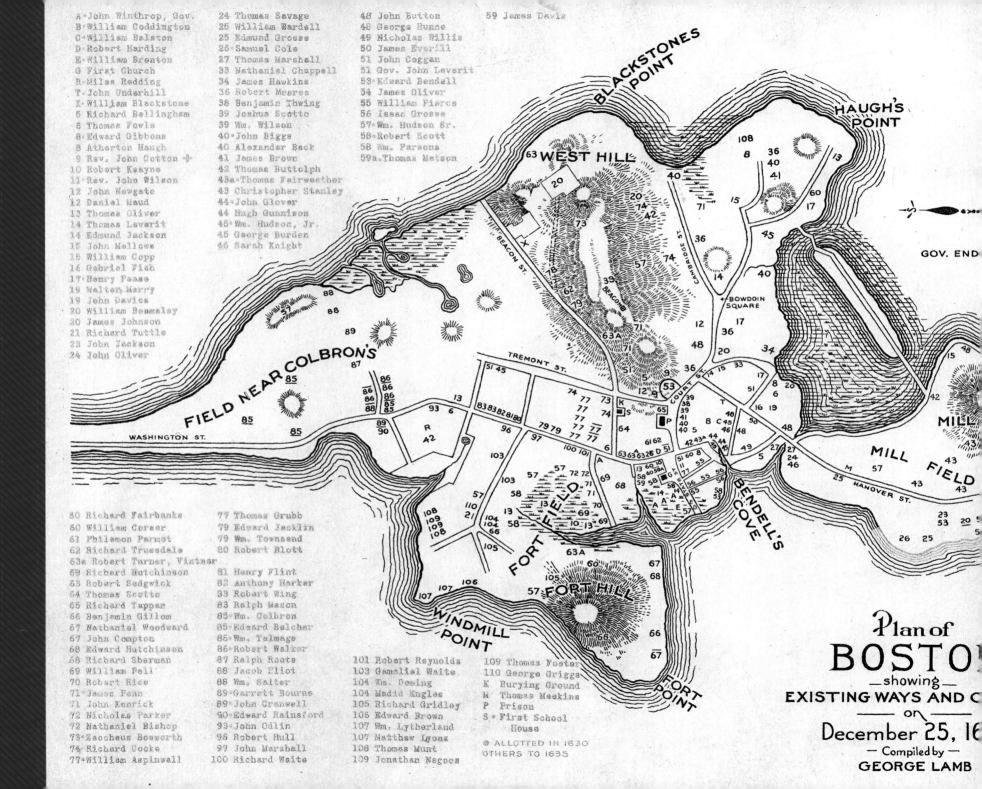

Plan of BOSTON showing EXISTING WAYS AND C[...] on December 25, 16[...] — Compiled by — GEORGE LAMB

ROOTS

IN THE EARLY 17TH CENTURY, Europeans did not know much about what is now the Boston area. In 1614, English captain John Smith, who had established Jamestown, Virginia, sailed on a voyage of exploration from Maine south to Cape Cod, Massachusetts, charting and making observations. When Smith returned to England, he described the area to Prince Charles, who was very pleased and named the region New England. In the years that followed, several ships sailing from England visited the Massachusetts coast.

1635 Map of Boston showing existing ways and owners. *Wikimedia Commons*

First Exploration

In 1606, the Plymouth Company was formed with the purpose of recruiting people to settle in America and making a profit for the company. Finally, after it reorganized in 1620 as the Council for New England, the company achieved its goal when 102 settlers landed at a site in Massachusetts they called Plymouth (about 40 miles south of Boston). During the 1620s, English colonists made further exploration and settlements along the coast, with varying success.

An attempted settlement at Weymouth (15 miles from Boston) in 1622 ended in failure due to unprepared colonists and inadequate supplies. By 1624, some of the Pilgrims had established posts at Hull (8 miles south of Boston) and Cape Ann (40 miles north of Boston). Quincy (about 10 miles south of Boston) was first settled in 1625, as was Salem (about 20 miles north of Boston). Around this time, a few men had settled on the islands and peninsula in Boston's inner harbor: David Thompson lived on Thompson Island, William Blackstone lived at Boston, Samuel Maverick lived on Noddle's Island (East Boston), and Thomas Walford at Charlestown. By 1628, Salem was a settlement of about 50 or 60 people, and by 1629 there were 350 people there.

Captain John Smith explored the New England coast in 1614, passing what would become Boston.

POCAHONTAS

The Massachusetts Bay Company

In 1628, the Plymouth Company granted a strip of land between the Merrimac and Charles Rivers to six men, who soon after formed a commercial venture called the Massachusetts Bay Company, which the King of England chartered and authorized to settle New England. Though the land was technically owned by England, this colony would not be governed by the English monarchy. It would be governed by the stockholders of the company, or "freemen," who would elect a governor, deputy governor, and assistants from their own company every year. Though one of the main reasons for this venture was clearly to make money, a paper

called "Reasons for the Plantation in New England" stated the number-one reason as "it will be a service to the Church of great consequence to carry the Gospell into those parts of the world."

In 1629, the Massachusetts Bay Company selected John Winthrop as its first governor and others as deputy governor and assistants, (representatives of the people). They were to hold a General Court several times a year to create laws and make rulings. Colonists were recruited to establish the colony. Unlike their predecessors, the Pilgrims at Plymouth, these colonists were not religious outcasts or exiles; they were members of the Church of England. Still, their settlement was to be a bold and difficult adventure. Leaving their comfortable and familiar homes in England for the unknown across the ocean was a huge step. At a farewell dinner among friends before departing

England, Governor Winthrop broke into tears and set the entire party to crying. Before they began their journey, members of the company published a declaration directed to fellow members of the Church of England in which they laid out the goals of their trip but also asked for prayers while they were in their "poor cottages in the wilderness."

Arrival in the New World

In the early spring of 1630, 17 vessels carrying 1,500 people along with a supply of pigs, sheep, goats, and horses, set sail for Massachusetts. The colonists also brought nails, glass, and iron works to use to construct buildings until they could make their own supplies. The ships arrived at different times between April and July 1630. Governor Winthrop's ship took 84 days to make the journey from England. Soon after their arrival, the governor and his men looked for a location for the capital. The governor's first home was a house on the north side of the Charles River at Charlestown, erected hastily by those who had arrived first. The majority of the settlers lived at first in tents and huts, which offered minimal shelter.

One of the settlers, Roger Clapp, wrote an account of life in the spring of 1630: "In our beginning, many were in great straits for want of provision for themselves and their little ones. Oh, the hunger that many suffered, and saw no hope in an eye of reason to be supplied, only by clams, and muscles, and fish. But bread was with many a very scarce thing, and flesh of all kinds as scarce. It was not accounted a strange thing in those days to drink water and to eat samp or hominy without butter or milk. Indeed it would have been a strange thing to see a piece of roast beef, mutton, or veal." At one point the desperate settlers traded an English puppy to the local Native Americans for a peck (a dry measurement equivalent to two gallons) of corn.

The settlers at Charlestown were not entirely impressed with the location they'd chosen. One of their main complaints was that there was only a freshwater spring, and it was not large enough or clean enough for their water needs. William Blackstone (or Blaxton) visited the new settlers and told them there was an excellent spring on his property, in what was then known as Blackstone's Neck. So it was that the settlers began to populate Shawmut, also known as Boston.

Among the proclamations the General Court issued at its first meetings in 1630 were a fine of £10 to anyone who allowed an Indian to use a gun. (A second offense would result in a fine and imprisonment.) Another order offered a reward to anyone who killed a wolf, a creature that endangered precious livestock. The court also issued an order giving a commission to anyone who set up a ferry between Boston and Charlestown: one penny for every person and one penny for every £100 of goods that were taken across on the ferry.

Boston's Geology

Boston's geography and geology are due in large part to the forces at play during the Ice Age. For example, Boston Harbor was created by moving glaciers wearing away the bedrock that underlies the land. The granite under the areas north and south of Boston is harder than the bedrock under the immediate Boston area, so those areas were not affected as much by the glaciers. As the glaciers eroded the bedrock, a valley was formed. When the glaciers melted and the sea level rose, this depression was filled with water, creating the harbor we know today.

The glaciers' movement was also responsible for creating the many drumlins (smooth-sloped, circular-shaped hills) in the Boston area, which are made up of glacial debris or till, clay-soil containing many pebbles and even boulders. Some of the islands in the Boston Harbor are actually drumlins. At the end of the Ice Age, when the glaciers melted and retreated north, they left behind sediment, sand, gravel, and larger rocks that had been frozen within the ice.

The Patron Saint of Boston

The story of Boston's name dates back to the seventh century AD in England, when a Saxon noble named Botolph (Old English name meaning "boat helper") was educated in an abbey in France. When an inspired Botolph returned to England, he received a land grant from King Onna to build a monastery in Lincolnshire in the East Anglia region of the country. This abbey and the village that grew around it became known as Botolphston.

After his death in 680, Botolph was sainted for his good works. In the years that followed, more than 60 English churches were dedicated to

St. Botolph. The name *Botolphston* was eventually corrupted into *Boston*, which is the name of a town about 130 miles north of London. Puritan settlers from this region of England wound up giving their settlement in the New World the same name.

St. Botolph is the patron saint of the US city of Boston, and the name can be found across the city. The St. Botolph District is a historic eight-block neighborhood there. A St. Botolph public housing apartment building sits on St. Botolph Street, and a St. Botolph Club for the arts was founded in Boston in 1880.

During the Ice Age, the glaciers carried large boulders, such as the Ship Rock in Peabody, to the Boston area and deposited them there.
Author's collection

Stratigraphy Game

Stratigraphy is the natural or artificial layering of the ground. Different layers of soil represent the different forces that were in play over time. Decaying twigs, leaves, and even animal remains make up the top, and often darkest and richest, layer of soil. Over the years, earthworms help make new soil, which is deposited over the older soil. New plants grow well in the topsoil because it is rich in organic material. The dirt below the surface, which was once at the top, has lost some of its nutrients. Beyond these top layers, soil holds clues to the past. Archaeologists use stratigraphy to help them date artifacts buried in soil. In this activity, you'll explore your local soil. If you live in Boston or other parts of the northern United States, you will try to find evidence of glacial activity.

ADULT SUPERVISION REQUIRED

YOU'LL NEED

★ Small shovel

★ Brick trowel

★ Ruler

★ Pad of paper

★ Pencil

First, ask an adult for permission to dig outside. Use a shovel to dig a hole that is at least 4 inches wide. Dig the hole as deep as you can, at least 8 inches deep if possible. Use the trowel to level one side of the hole so it is relatively flat. Now look at the cross section (view from the side) of soil you just revealed. See if you can identify different layers of soil by the soil colors. How many different layers did you reveal?

Use the pad to sketch what you see. Measure and record the depth of each layer, give each layer a color name (for example, black, dark chocolate, milk chocolate, mustard, or gray), and describe it as fine, rocky, or coarse. You can also note how it feels in your hand—gritty, dry, moist, claylike, and so on.

If you live in the northern United States and see sandy, light-colored soil a few inches beneath the surface, chances are good that this layer was a deposit from retreating glaciers. Also, any smooth pebbles you excavate might be the product of glaciers or perhaps of the waves of an ancient ocean or lake in your area millions of years ago.

BOSTON'S GEOGRAPHY

BOSTON'S GEOGRAPHY HAS undergone more changes than almost any other city's in the history of the world. The topography and shape of modern Boston would be unrecognizable to a colonist visiting from the past. When it was first settled, the city was only 783 acres in size. The Boston of 1630 was situated on a small, irregularly shaped peninsula reachable from the mainland by a very narrow neck two blocks long by mere feet wide.

As with many of the country's coastal colonial cities, landfill was used to increase Boston's size over the years, and leveling its high ground helped create a more easily navigable city. Over the course of the years, landfill was added both east and west to massively increase the size of the city, completely transforming its geography. Areas that have been filled in since the early 19th century include West Cove, South Cove, East Cove, Mill Pond, South Boston, South Bay, and Back Bay. Landfill was even used to create Logan Airport.

Boston's size grew even larger when its borders were expanded to the west, into suburbs such as Roxbury, Mattapan, Dorchester, and Hyde Park. By 1893, Boston's size was 23,700 acres, and today it is 33,989 acres.

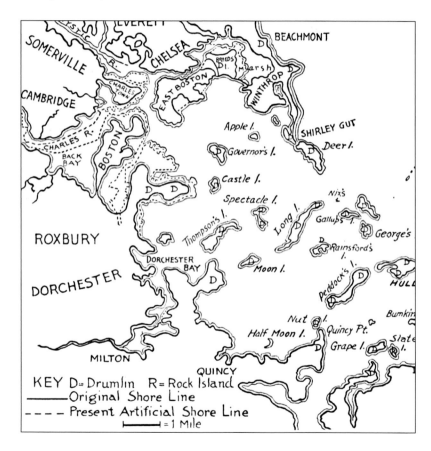

Much of present-day Boston sits on landfill. This 1920s map shows the outline of the original Boston area.
Author's collection

John Winthrop

John Winthrop, son of Adam and Anne Winthrop, was born in 1588 in Edwardston, England, about 60 miles northeast of London. As a child, he lived at Groton Manor, the estate of his father's family, which was granted to them by King Henry VIII. Young Winthrop was precocious and enrolled at Trinity College in 1602 at the age of 14. Winthrop may have been extremely bright, but in his mind he was "wild and dissolute" until finally, he said, "I fell into a lingering fever which took away the comforts of my life . . . and, being deprived of my youthful joys, I betook myself to God."

Winthrop's education was interrupted by his marriage to Mary Forth at the age of 17 and the birth of his son John Jr. (future governor of Connecticut) at the age of 18. Winthrop next opened a law practice and soon became a justice of the peace. His wife died in 1615 and he quickly remarried, but his second wife died giving birth a year later. He married a third time in 1618, to Margaret Tyndal (daughter of a knight), who bore eight children, four of whom wound up in New England.

Ironically, when Winthrop's eldest son wanted to sail to New England with a party of settlers in 1627, his father discouraged him. Instead, John Jr. went on a 14-month-long voyage to places as far away as Turkey. When he returned to England in the summer of 1629, he learned to his surprise that his father was about to depart for New England himself. John Winthrop Sr. had been employed in England's Parliament, but in 1629 he found himself out of work when the king dissolved Parliament.

Winthrop was ready for a new adventure, and managing Groton Manor was expensive. After being appointed as governor of the Massachusetts Bay Colony in 1629, Winthrop left England with two of his sons while his wife and two other sons remained in England until they could sell the family estate. Personal tragedy marred the start of the family's American life. Soon after Winthrop's arrival, his son Henry drowned in a creek near Salem. His wife Margaret finally arrived at Boston in November 1631, but their baby daughter Anne had died at sea.

What's in a Name?

The name *Massachusetts* comes from the Algonquin Massachusett tribe, members of which Captain John Smith encountered when he landed in the area in 1614. The name means "great hills place" or, more precisely, "at or near the great hills." The hills in question are the Blue Hills near Milton, about 15 miles south of Boston. The highest point among the hills, which are now part of Blue Hills Reservation (a state park), is Great Blue Hill, at 635 feet. Great Blue Hill may pale in comparison to the mountains in the western part of the state, but it is the second-highest hill in the Boston area, so to the natives it was a majestic sight. The natives named the bay *Massachusett*, and the colonists pluralized the name and gave it to their new colony.

Chances are, wherever you live in the United States, there are nearby place names that were inspired by Native American words. Look at a detailed local map and see if you can identify names with Native American origins. Check not only towns and villages but also rivers, mountains, counties, and even streets. Some of the country's most well-known cities have Native American names, such as Chattanooga and Tuscaloosa. Which tribes lived in your area in centuries past? See what research reveals. You might be surprised at what you find.

EARLY BOSTON

FROM THE VERY START, the young settlement of Boston thrived and grew, as did a neighboring settlement called Newtown, later to be known as Cambridge. The settlers built homes, churches, and a windmill and set up a colonial government. Soon more settlers arrived. Before long, a ferry began operation and the settlers founded a college. By 1640, Boston was one of the largest and most important settlements in the New World.

Southeast view of Boston circa 1730s–1750s.

Buying Blackstone's Boston

The General Court held its first meeting in October 1630 in Boston. In November, the governor and his deputy and their assistants moved to Boston from Charlestown. The colonists built homes and laid out streets, but the land still belonged to William Blackstone even though he had no official grant or deed. The General Court decided to make his ownership formal and in 1633 granted Blackstone 50 acres of land. In 1634, the inhabitants of Boston purchased most of the property from Blackstone for the price of six shillings per household. Under the deal, Blackstone (who lived with his wife, a son, and a daughter) got to keep six acres of land where his home was located. He bought some cows with the money he received and worked in his orchard and gardens. Blackstone eventually left Boston and moved to what is now Rhode Island, becoming the first European settler to make a home there.

The Governor Almost Lived in Cambridge

In 1630, a new town was settled across the Charles River from Boston, between Watertown and Charlestown. Deputy Governor Thomas Dudley and other settlers built the first houses there in 1631. The settlement was first called The New Towne, then New Town and Newtown, until 1638, when the General Court ordered that it be called Cambridge.

All the assistants agreed they would build houses in Cambridge, but only two of them actually did—Dudley and Simon Bradstreet (both future governors). As the story goes, Governor Winthrop built a house at Cambridge but then changed his mind when he saw that none of the other assistants were building theirs. He took his house down and erected it in Boston (and was scolded for doing so). By the end of 1631, only eight people were living in Cambridge. In 1632, around the same time that land was being divided into lots, the residents agreed to build a fence around New Town. Anyone whose property it crossed was responsible for repairing any damage to the fence.

Soon after the residents finished building the fence, a list was made of all the residents' names and how much fencing they were responsible for. The resident with the largest portion of fence on his property, 70 rods (one rod equals 16½ feet), was the future governor of Massachusetts Bay Colony, John Haynes, Esq. A windmill was built at what is now the south end of Ash Street to grind corn, but it was moved to Boston in 1632 because of unfavorable winds.

The first constable was appointed in 1632. By 1634, Cambridge was apparently thriving, as described in a book written by William Wood: "This place was first intended for a city; but, upon more serious consideration, it was thought not so fit, being too far from the sea. . . . This is one of the neatest and best compacted towns in New England, having many fair structures, with many handsome contrived streets. The inhabitants, most of them, are very rich, and well stored with cattle of all sorts."

Early Cambridge was just as important as Boston. The General Court, which had moved from Charlestown to Boston toward the end of 1630, relocated to Cambridge in 1634 and remained there until 1636, when it returned to Boston. The General Court again held its meetings in Cambridge in 1637 until it returned permanently to Boston in 1638. Early elections of the governor and magistrates (also known as assistants, representatives of the Massachusetts Bay Company) were held in Cambridge, under an oak tree on the north side of the Boston Common. The 1637 election was a scene of some turmoil as one candidate delayed the election by protesting over a petition he wanted read and the other candidate protested the delay. Things were at a standstill until one official climbed onto the bough of the tree and made a speech imploring the people to come together with common purpose to carry on with the election of the governor and the rest of the Massachusetts government. The people agreed and began to chant "Election! Election!" and the election went forward.

The Earthquake of 1638

On June 1, 1638, New England experienced a great earthquake that could be felt for hundreds of miles in Massachusetts and Connecticut. The quake, the first recorded in the colonies, was preceded by a low rumbling sound like distant thunder that became louder and stronger as the quake began to be felt. Dishes and pewter vessels clattered from shelves, stone walls buckled, tops of chimneys broke off, and the citizens of Boston steadied themselves, grabbing what they could to prevent themselves from falling over. According to town records, men working in fields threw down their tools and ran "with gastly, terrified looks." The ships in Boston Harbor shook. The quake lasted for four minutes, and another, less severe quake occurred a half hour later. Aftershocks came for the next three weeks. A 19th-century historian named William T. Brigham wrote of the 1638 tremor, "So little interest did natural phenomena excite in those days—unless indeed they could be connected to some poor witch, or used as weapons by the belligerent clergy—that the scanty records remaining do not give much information of any value."

Mrs. Sherman's Pig

In 1637, a young pig got loose from Mrs. Sherman, a poor Boston widow, and it wandered around the city until someone brought it to the wealthy Captain Robert Keayne, who lived at the corner of Washington and State Streets. Keayne had the town crier advertise the newly found pig and try to find the rightful owner, but with no success. He kept and raised the new pig with one of his own pigs.

After a year, Keayne killed his old pig. At this point, Mrs. Sherman came forward, claiming the slaughtered pig was in fact hers, and that Keayne knew it was hers and killed it on purpose. She took her complaint to the church elders, who dismissed it. She next took Keayne to court, but the jury

Harvard College as seen in 1726.

found in his favor and awarded him three pounds in costs. Then Keayne sued her for defamation and got a verdict and an award of £40.

A sympathetic London merchant named George Story took up the woman's case and claimed that one of the captain's witnesses had lied in court. The General Court took up the case next. After seven days of testimony, it was time for the magistrates and deputies (delegates from the various towns) to vote. The rules required a majority

vote by each group for a decision. Of the 30 deputies, 15 voted for Mrs. Sherman and 8 for Captain Keayne, with 7 abstentions. Of the 9 magistrates, 2 were for Sherman and 7 for Keayne. It was a stalemate, even though the combined majority was for Mrs. Sherman.

The unsatisfactory outcome of this "Sow Business," as it became known, caused quite a stir and in 1644 ultimately led to the assistants and deputies being separated into two houses, parliamentary style, each with veto power over the other. Mrs. Sherman's lost pig was the origin of the modern form of our Congress, House of Representatives, and Senate.

Eventually, Captain Keayne decided to give the young pig back to Mrs. Sherman.

Harvard Is Founded

In 1636, only six years after Boston was settled, the Massachusetts government called for the founding of a college. Leaders voted to give a sum of £400 to that cause. They selected Newtown as the site of the college as it was "a place very pleasant and accommodate." A committee of 12 important officials, including Governor Winthrop, was named to ensure that the job would be done. In 1638, Newtown's name was changed to Cambridge in honor of the university in England where many leading Massachusetts colonists had received their education. Classes began that same year, and in 1639, the new school was named Harvard after the Reverend John Harvard, who had died in 1638 of consumption and bequeathed £779 toward the establishment of a college in Massachusetts colony. He also donated his library of 320 books.

The college's first leader was Nathaniel Eaton, appointed as "master" in 1637. He had the great responsibility of overseeing the education of the students, managing donations, and getting buildings constructed. By all accounts, he seems to have been a failure at his mission. In 1639, he was accused of mistreating the students by giving them scanty and inedible food rations, and of beating his assistant. The General Court dismissed Eaton, fined him £66, and ordered him to pay another £30 to his assistant. He was excommunicated from the local church and fled to Virginia and then England.

Other than this unfortunate incident, the college was off to a good start. In 1639, the first printing press north of Mexico arrived at Cambridge thanks to Harvard's academic reputation. In 1640, the Reverend Henry Dunster became president of Harvard. The first graduating class of nine men received their diplomas in 1642, and they were the first in British America to graduate from an American college.

Donations from a variety of people and for a variety of different amounts began to come in as the school's reputation grew. Not all the early donations were money. Some were oddball items, such as sheep, cotton fabric, and a pewter drinking vessel.

Though it had no religious affiliations, in its early years Harvard was run by several members of the clergy and also taught many future members of the clergy. The most famous of its early presidents was Increase Mather, who ran the school from 1685 to 1701.

Two Ferries and a Bridge

When Boston was first settled, the only way to get there from inland was over the narrow, 40-yard-wide neck that crossed the harbor and led to the town. Though it might have been OK for people living west of Boston, it was especially

BOSTON'S LOSS IS RHODE ISLAND'S GAIN

When the college-educated Roger Williams arrived in Boston at the age of 24, he found it hard to fit in due to his separation from the Church of England. He wound up in Salem, where he taught a group of Separatists. His views were offensive to the government of Massachusetts. In 1635, the General Court met in Boston and banished him for "new and dangerous opinions, against the authority of magistrates." He purchased land from Native Americans in what is now Rhode Island and created a settlement in what he called Providence Plantation, a place that offered religious freedom. This promise drew many others seeking shelter from persecution, including Anne Hutchinson and other religious dissidents fleeing from Massachusetts.

inconvenient for those living just north of Boston, who had to make a detour west and south to reach the neck even though Boston was within their sights just across the Charles River.

In 1631, a few months after the General Court called for someone to start up a ferry service, Edward Converse established a ferry between Charlestown and Boston—the first ferry to operate in the colonies. He was allowed to charge two pence for each person who crossed and one penny apiece for parties of two or more people. In 1633, Richard Brown was authorized to start a ferry across the Charles River, and in 1635, another was opened from Charlestown to Windmill Hill in Boston.

In 1637, the General Court gave Edward Converse the right to operate the sole ferry carrying passengers and cattle from Boston to Charlestown for three years, for the rent of £40 a year. But Converse was not the most attentive ferry operator, and in 1638, the court ordered him to man two boats, one on each side of the river. When Converse's contract ended in 1640, the court decided it would no longer allow private citizens to operate the Boston–Charlestown ferry and instead gave that right to Harvard College (which was directly adjacent to the ferry). The college used the ferry revenue to help pay for the cost of operating the school.

Ferry operation was not always pleasant. In 1648, two ferry operators complained to the General Court that passengers were sometimes disorderly and refused to pay their fares, or paid in damaged wampum (Native American shell money). They also complained that soldiers and their horses insisted on riding for free and asked that they be reimbursed for those trips. The court understood and said that the ferrymen could collect their fares before departing, that wampum had to be in good condition and properly strung, and that except in extraordinary cases, only magistrates and deputies of the court were allowed to ride for free.

Though ferries were convenient, a bridge would be even more useful. In 1662, a tremendous undertaking was completed—the construction of the "Great Bridge," made of wood and planks, between Boston and Cambridge (located near the site of the current Anderson Memorial Bridge near Harvard Stadium). Until the late 18th century, these options were the only ways to cross the river.

Early Boston Laws

Regulations in 17th-century Boston were very strict and banned behaviors that went against Puritan values. Over the years, regulations targeted a variety of different evils. In 1631, people were encouraged to get rid of any dice, cards, or gaming tables they may have had in their homes. Even sweets were suspect. According to colony records of November 1637, "No person shall sell any cakes or bunns either in the market . . . or elsewhere, upon pain of ten shillings fine, provided, that this order shall not extend to such cakes as shall be made for any burial, or marriage, or such like special occasion."

In 1639, several people filed a court complaint that Captain Keayne, a shopkeeper in Boston, was making extremely high profits on the foreign goods he imported and sold. He was convicted and fined. He had to plead his case before church elders, during which he wept openly and admitted his guilt. His friends, however, defended him, saying that some business ventures were losing propositions, so why should others not be winning ones? Otherwise, how could he make a living?

In 1647, a table game called shovelboard (a relative of modern shuffleboard) was banned from inns as being too likely to cause drinking and commotion. In 1651, the government prohibited dancing in taverns, and in 1664, banned "rudely singing" in taverns.

Keeping the strictest order at night was very important to the city fathers. In 1662, regulations stated that constables on night duty were to walk in pairs, a younger one always paired with an older one. Constables had to be model citizens and not use "uncleane or corrupt language, nor unmanerlye or unbeseming tearmes."

As they made their rounds, constables who saw lights on in a home after 10:00 PM were to "make discreett inquiry, whether there be a warrantable cause" and they were also to be on the lookout for excessive noise or disorderly conduct in any house, and inquire as to the reason. If they find "men are danceing, drinckeing, Singinge vainlie," they were to order them to stop at risk of punishment. Likewise, if they spotted anyone walking around after 10:00 PM, they were to "modestly demand" the reason. If the walkers appeared to be up to no good, the constables were to order them to return to their homes immediately. If they refused to explain what they were doing outside or refused to return home when asked, they were to be detained until morning.

Crime in early Puritan Boston was met with a stern hand. Josiah Plastow's punishment for stealing four baskets of corn from the local Native Americans was to give them eight baskets of corn and pay a fine. John Wedgwood was put in stocks for being in the company of drunks. Robert Coles was fined £10 and made to stand with a paper on his back that said DRUNKARD in large letters.

Early Boston Churches

Boston's first settlers were very religious, and building a church was an important step in making the new settlement their permanent home.

The First Church in Boston was a wooden building built in 1632, and rebuilt larger in 1639. This building burned down in 1711 and was replaced with a brick building, which became known as the Old Brick Church. By 1649, the town was too big for just one church, and a second, known as the Old North Church, was built in North Square in 1650. It burned down in 1676 and was rebuilt in 1677. The church stood until British general William Howe had his troops demolish it during the Siege of Boston in 1775. This is not to be confused with the historic Old North Church that was built in 1723 and is still standing today.

Another early church, the Old South Church on Marlborough Street, was built in 1669. British soldiers destroyed its interior in 1775 and used the building as a riding school for their horses. The church was repaired in 1782. Other early Boston churches were the small King's Chapel, an Episcopal church erected in 1688, and the first Baptist Church in Boston (which was built in 1679). The first Catholic church in the city was not built until 1801; there are now almost 300 Catholic churches in Boston.

The most famous of Boston's early preachers were the Mathers, Cotton and Increase, a father and son duo. They were descendants of Richard Mather, who arrived in New England in 1635 and was the preacher at a church in Dorchester, Massachusetts. One of Richard's sons, Samuel, gave a sermon upon the opening of the Old North Church in Boston in 1650. Samuel returned to England, and 14 years later, in 1664, his brother Increase was ordained as minister at the Old North Church. Increase's son Cotton was ordained in 1684, and the two men preached side by side for 39 years. Increase died in 1723 and his son just five years later. While they were well known at the time, both men would gain their lasting fame (or infamy) not from their church services and sermons but from their roles in the witch trials of the late 17th century.

Banning Native Americans

Between 1675 and 1678, the Massachusetts colonists were engaged in a bloody war with the local Native Americans. This war, called King Philip's War after a local Indian chief, was tragic on both sides, causing the loss of life and property throughout Massachusetts. One of the most devastating events of the war was an ambush on English militia near Deerfield in western Massachusetts in September 1675, resulting in the death of 57 colonists. One month later, the Massachusetts General Court passed a law that made it illegal for any Indian to enter Boston or for anyone to offer one shelter. The law was eventually repealed in 2005, 330 years later.

That was not the only repercussion for the Native Americans. In the winter of 1675–76, peaceful local Indians were rounded up and forcibly taken to islands in the Boston Harbor, where they were jailed. As many as 1,000 natives were relocated to the islands, and historians believe about half of them died of starvation, disease, or exposure.

Old North Church.

Old South Church.

John Goodwin and the Witch

Most 17th-century American colonists were quite superstitious, and the Puritans of Massachusetts were certainly no exception. They believed in a variety of supernatural forces, both harmless and evil. One story told of a Boston man named Joseph Beacon, who one night in May 1687 had a terrifying vision of his brother, who lived in London at that time. In the dream, the brother told Beacon he had been murdered. Beacon later found out that his brother had in fact died on that very day, in the same manner his brother had described in the vision.

Cotton Mather.

One of the strangest and most frightening times in New England's history was the witch hunt of the late 17th century. Though accusations of witchcraft had occurred earlier in the 1600s, the witch frenzy began in 1688. It started when the 13-year-old daughter of a Boston man named John Goodwin questioned the family laundress (an Irish Catholic woman named Ann Glover who claimed to speak Gaelic and know little English) about some missing linen that she suspected the woman had stolen from the family. As the story went, the washerwoman's mother, who was a suspected witch, was angry that her daughter had been accused of this crime and placed a spell on the girl. The girl had severe seizures and many strange and violent pains, which puzzled and concerned her family. Before long, one of the girl's sisters and two of her brothers also had the same symptoms.

The children's symptoms kept changing. Sometimes they were deaf, sometimes mute, and sometimes blind. People said that the children's bodies could twist and turn in odd ways, their jaws falling wide open, their tongues drooping out of their mouths, and their joints popping. The doctor who examined the children concluded that witchcraft was the cause. Authorities arrested the washerwoman's mother and searched her house. They found several puppets or dolls inside, stuffed with goat hair. During the woman's trial, these puppets were brought as evidence. Supposedly, she admitted that she wet her finger with her saliva and smeared it on the puppets to cause the children's misery. When one of the dolls was handed to the suspected witch, one of the children (who were all in the courtroom) had a seizure. Six doctors examined the woman and ruled her to be sane. She was then sentenced to death and executed.

After the supposed witch's death, Reverend Cotton Mather of the Old North Church took the eldest girl to his house and observed her. Based on the Goodwin story and his observations of the girl's behavior, the animal noises she made, and her attempts to recover and lead a normal life, in 1689 he published *Memorable Providences Relating to Witchcrafts and Possessions—A Faithful Account of the Many Wonderful and Surprising Things, That*

Have Befallen Several Bewitched and Possessed Persons in New England. All of Boston's ministers signed and certified the preface of this book, which reads more like a modern-day horror story than a true tale. In the preface, the ministers made their case for the existence of witches. They wrote, "Though it be folly to impute every dubious accident, or unwonted effect of Providence, to Witchcraft, yet there are some things which cannot be excepted against, but must be ascribed hither."

This book became very popular, and before long all of New England was riled up about witches. When suspected cases of witchcraft broke out in nearby Salem in 1692 (in the home of a minister who happened to own Mather's witchcraft book), the witch hunt became an epidemic and fear triumphed over reason. When all was said and done, 20 people had been found guilty of witchcraft and executed, including 14 women. Dozens of people had been accused or suspected of being witches, and many others had claimed to be the victims of witchcraft.

Cotton Mather went on to write *The Wonders of the Invisible World*, published in 1693. He used the book, which was based on the Salem witch trials, to defend his full-fledged assault on witchcraft. It included accounts of some of the women who had been tried. By mid-1693, however, the madness was over and no more suspected witches were brought to trial.

Meanwhile, a Boston merchant named Robert Calef had had enough of the witchcraft nonsense. He felt that Mather had stirred up an unjustified witchcraft frenzy, and started working on a book to

The Wonders of the Invisible World:

Being an Account of the

TRYALS

OF

Several Witches,

Lately Excuted in

NEW-ENGLAND:

And of several remarkable Curiosities therein Occurring.

Together with,

I. Obſervations upon the Nature, the Number, and the Operations of the Devils.

II. A ſhort Narrative of a late outrage committed by a knot of Witches in *Swede-Land*, very much reſembling, and ſo far explaining, that under which *New-England* has laboured.

III. Some Councels directing a due Improvement of the Terrible things lately done by the unuſual and amazing Range of *Evil-Spirits* in *New-England*.

IV. A brief Diſcourſe upon thoſe *Temptations* which are the more ordinary Devices of Satan.

By COTTON MATHER.

Publiſhed by the Special Command of his EXCELLENCY the Governcur of the Province of the *Maſſachuſetts-Bay* in *New-England*.

Printed firſt, at *Boſton* in *New-England*; and Reprinted at *London*, for *John Dunton*, at the *Raven* in the *Poultry*. 1693.

Cotton Mather's book, *The Wonders of the Invisible World*.

expose the flaws in Mather's theories. After several years, in 1697, he finished writing the book, *More Wonders of the Invisible World*. But Calef could not find a Boston publisher willing to print it, thanks to the influence of the Mathers. It was finally published in London in 1700. Though it had been a few years since the witchcraft excitement, Calef's attack infuriated the Mathers. Increase Mather publicly burned a copy of the book, and Cotton Mather's friends angrily wrote a book in response, titled *Some Few Remarks, upon a Scandalous Book, Against the Government and Ministry of New-England*.

Capturing Captain Kidd

In May 1699, the notorious pirate-hunter turned pirate Captain William Kidd had just returned to North America from a raid of an Arabian ship called the *Quedagh Merchant*. The *Quedagh Merchant* was just one of several ships Kidd had commandeered while out at sea, but it had the richest treasure of them all. Kidd left the valuable ship in the care of his first mate off the coast of what is now the Dominican Republic and sailed toward New York in a smaller vessel to test the waters before attempting to bring the treasure back. While Kidd thought he was justified in seizing that and other ships, he started to realize that the English government that had sent him to hunt pirates was not of the same opinion.

Concerned, he wrote to the Earl of Bellomont, governor of New England and the man who had sent him to hunt pirates, and expressed his innocence. Bellomont was in Boston at the time, and Kidd wished to meet with the Earl in person. Bellomont reassured him:

I have advised with his Majesty's Council, and showed them this letter, and they are of opinion if your case be so clear as you have said, you may safely come hither and be equipped or fitted out to go to fetch the other ship; and I make no doubt but to obtain the King's pardon for you and those few men you have left, which I understand have been faithful to you, and refused, as well as you, to dishonor the Commission you had from England. I assure you on my word and honor I will nicely perform what I have promised, and not to meddle with the least bitt of whatever goods or treasure you bring here, but that the same shall be left with such trusty persons as the Council shall advise until I receive orders from England how it shall be disposed of.

Though the bulk of his treasure lay with the *Quedagh Merchant*, Kidd still had a sizable treasure with him, which he decided to stash despite Bellomont's letter, just to be safe. He anchored his boat near Gardiner's Island, a small island east of Long Island, and went ashore. He buried the treasure under an old oak tree, swearing the island's owner, John Gardiner, to secrecy.

Feeling confident, Kidd picked up his wife and children and sailed for Boston. He arrived there on July 1, 1699, and stayed in the fancy lodgings of one of Boston's most popular citizens, Duncan Campbell. Two days after he arrived at Boston, Captain Kidd was summoned to appear before

Lord Bellomont to give an account of his voyage and ship seizures. Kidd asked Bellomont to give him until the next day, July 4, to write down his adventures. On the fourth, Kidd appeared before Bellomont, said he had not begun writing yet, and asked for more time. Bellomont grew impatient. He had orders from the English government to arrest Kidd and had delayed enforcing them. On July 6, Bellomont had Captain Kidd arrested and thrown in prison. At first Kidd was kept in the prison-keeper's house, but 10 days later he was thrown into the gloomy and heavily fortified stone prison located on Prison Lane (now Court Street), between School and Tremont Streets.

When Kidd was arrested, the authorities opened his wife's personal trunk and found and seized a silver tankard, a silver mug, a silver porringer (a bowl with a handle), silverware, and 260 pieces of eight (coins). His wife protested, claiming those items were hers and hers alone. She requested they be returned to her, and they were.

The authorities wanted desperately to know where the treasure was. Finally, Captain Kidd relented and told them that John Gardiner would be able to tell them where on his island the treasure was buried. Since Gardiner wanted to cooperate, he went to the secret spot, dug up the treasure, and brought most of it with him to Boston. The treasure included 1,111 ounces of gold, 2,353 ounces of silver, 17¾ ounces of rubies, exotic fabrics, and a bushel of nutmeg and cloves. The authorities also seized 57 bags of sugar from Kidd's ship.

When Gardiner returned home from Boston, the story goes that as he unpacked his bag, a diamond dropped out. He wanted to send it to Boston, but his wife told him to keep it after all the trouble Captain Kidd had caused him.

Meanwhile, Kidd wanted permission to go to Hispaniola to retrieve the *Quedagh Merchant* and its £50,000 of treasure. Bellomont refused. Then, on July 17, word reached Boston that the first mate had taken off with the treasure and burned the ship. Archaeologists found the wreck of the ship in 2007, but to this day nobody has found the treasure. Kidd remained a prisoner in Boston until he was taken to England in April 1700, and there he remained in prison until his trial in May 1701. He was found guilty of murdering one of his crewmen by striking him on the head with a bucket and was hanged for that crime, not for piracy.

Newspapers and Printing

Massachusetts was a printing pioneer. The first printing press in the country was set up in Cambridge in 1638, and the first printing press in Boston began operating in about 1675. The *Boston News-Letter* was the first newspaper published in North America. It was printed in April 1704 by Bartholomew Green, who ran his operation from a small wooden building on Newbury Street near the Old Meeting House.

News traveled very slowly in the 18th century. The entire cover page of the first issue (which was only two pages) featured a political story from England that had been published in a British newspaper four months earlier, in December 1703. The second page had more news from England

The Beacon Hill beacon as it appeared in the late 18th century.

along with a few local-interest items, including the big local story: the arrival of a ship from Virginia whose captain told the governor of Massachusetts that he had been chased off Block Island by a French pirate ship. The governor was very concerned and quickly organized a search party in just four hours. He sent a ship with 70 men to search for the alleged pirate ship.

The first *Boston News-Letter* also contained notices about which ships were sailing from different North American ports. Other "news" included a brief story about the Reverend Pemberton preaching an excellent sermon on Thessalonians 4:11, and a story about a judge of the admiralty being appointed for Massachusetts, New Hampshire, and Rhode Island.

There was also an advertisement telling readers that the paper would be weekly and that "all Persons who have any Houses, Lands, Tenements, Farms, Ships, Vessels, Goods, Wares or Merchandizes, etc. to be Sold, or Let; or Servants Runaway, or Goods Stole or Lost; may have the same inserted at a Reasonable Rate." The *Boston News-Letter* ran until 1776.

Other newspapers soon followed, including the *Boston Gazette* (1719), the *New England Courant* (1721), the *New England Weekly Journal* (1727), the *Weekly Rehearsal* (1731), the *Boston Weekly Post-Boy* (1734), and the *Boston Evening-Post* (1735).

The Beacon Hill Beacon

One of Boston's earliest and longest-lasting landmarks was a pole. A tall beacon was erected at the top of Centry Hill (now Beacon Hill) in 1634. The General Court of the Colony called for the construction of the signal: "It is ordered that there shalbe forth with a beacon sett on the centry hill at Boston, to give norice to the country of any danger and that there shall be a ward of one pson kept there from the first of April to the last of Septr., & that upon the discov'y of any danger, the beacon shalbe fired, an allarum given, as also messengers presently sent by that towne where the danger is discov'ed, to the other townes within their jirisdiccon."

The beacon consisted of a tall pole rising from a stone and wood foundation. At a height of 65 feet was an iron arm with an iron pot that could hold burning tar to create a signal fire. Because local citizens could see the beacon from a good distance, it could warn them of any danger. It is not clear how often the beacon was actually used, but one of its early uses was to warn of possible attacks by local Native Americans.

The beacon stood atop the hill until it was felled during a storm in November 1789. In 1790, it was replaced by a 60-foot-high cement-covered brick column designed by Charles Bulfinch. The new monument was topped with a large gilded wooden eagle.

America's Oldest Lighthouse

Lighthouses serve a critically important purpose: to help ships navigating near the coast avoid dangerous islands, reefs, and rocks that can cause wrecks and loss of life. Since Boston Harbor has

The Boston Light, built 1716, as seen in 1729.

many such obstacles, a lighthouse had to be built as soon as possible. The government of Massachusetts selected the seven-acre Little Brewster Island (nine miles from Boston) for the location of the Boston Light, which was constructed in 1716. This lighthouse was a 60-foot-high circular stone tower lit by candles. The tower was damaged by candle fires in 1720 and 1751 and by a storm in 1723, and was rebuilt each time. The Americans set fire to the lighthouse three times during the Revolutionary War when Boston was occupied by the British, and then the British blew it up in June 1776. Boston Light was rebuilt after the war, in 1783, as a 75-foot-high tower.

Many improvements were made in the years since, including a revolving mechanism to allow the light to appear to be flashing. The tower was raised to 89 feet and a revolving lens was installed in 1859. Various fog signals were used over the years, including a fog cannon, a whistle, and a steam siren. The lighthouse was finally electrified in 1948. Boston Light became a national historic landmark in 1964. In 1998, its light became the last in the country to be fully automated, and today it is the only lighthouse in the United States that is still manned. Little Brewster Island is open to visitors, who can climb the 76 steps to the top and enjoy the view from the country's oldest continually used lighthouse.

Ben Bids Bye-Bye to Boston

Though Benjamin Franklin is closely associated with Philadelphia, he spent the first 17 years of his life in Boston. The son of a soap boiler and candlemaker, he was born in 1706 in a house on Milk Street. After a few years, the Franklins moved to the corner of Hanover and Union Streets.

Franklin showed little interest in working in his father's trade, and after 12-year-old Benjamin rejected several other trades, his father convinced him to work as an apprentice to his older brother James, who was a printer. The younger Franklin did odd jobs and learned the trade for no pay, under the harsh eye of his brother. The brothers had many disputes, and their father often resolved them in Ben's favor. This made James resent his brother more, and he even beat Ben on occasion.

Benjamin became interested in poetry and began to write some verse. His brother, seeing an opportunity to make some money, encouraged young Franklin. Ben wrote *The Lighthouse Tragedy*, a ballad about the true story of a sea captain named Captain Worthilake who drowned with his two daughters. His brother printed the poem and had Ben sell it on the streets of Boston. Ben was encouraged by the brisk sales, but his father ridiculed his efforts and he gave up poetry.

When James Franklin began a newspaper, the *New England Courant*, in 1721, Benjamin desperately wanted to write for it, but his job was to deliver the newspapers to customers. Writing "wretched stuff," as Benjamin later called his poetry, had been fine, but he knew if he tried to submit a serious piece to his brother, it would be rejected. So young Benjamin did the logical thing: he wrote an anonymous article and slipped it under his brother's office door. To Ben's delight, his brother printed the article! Ben continued to write more unsigned articles.

Soon after the newspaper debuted, James Franklin found himself in trouble with the law. The *Courant* was an outspoken newspaper. Its articles attacked a variety of government officials for one reason or another, and also attacked the Boston clergy for supporting smallpox inoculation. To punish James for the continuing attacks, the government threw him in prison for a month, and 15-year-old Benjamin became the newspaper's publisher. James Franklin was later released from prison with the stern warning that he could no longer publish the *New England Courant*.

James wanted to keep Ben's name on the newspaper masthead, but he worried that the authorities might think he, and not his apprentice brother, was the real publisher. James released Ben from his official apprenticeship and made him sign a secret, personal document that gave James full control over Ben, who was not paid for his work. "A very flimsy scheme it was; however, it was immediately executed, and the paper went on accordingly under my name for several months," Franklin wrote in his autobiography.

It was too much for Ben. By the fall of 1723, he told his brother he was leaving the newspaper. James proceeded to visit every other printing house in Boston and demand that they not hire his brother. That was the final straw. Ben felt like a prisoner, and to make matters worse, his father sided with James. Ben realized that if he tried to leave the newspaper, James would stop him. After selling some of his beloved books to raise money, with the help of a friend he got passage on a ship and sailed to New York. From there he would travel to Philadelphia and gain the fame that lasts to this day.

The Duel to End All Duels

On the evening of July 3, 1728, two young merchants named Benjamin Woodbridge (age 19) and Henry Phillips (age 23) were drinking and playing games at Luke Vardy's Royal Exchange Tavern on King Street. The two apparently had an argument that became serious, and they decided to settle their quarrel once and for all around 10:00 PM on the Boston Common, near the Powder House.

Each man was alone, and each had a sword. They fought, and Phillips ran his sword completely through Woodbridge's chest. Woodbridge fell dead on the spot.

It was the first duel in Boston history. The fallen man's body was found early the next morning and taken to the home of his business partner. Many dignitaries and merchants attended Woodbridge's

FRANKLIN AND THE MIRACLE OF COMPOUND INTEREST

Boston and Philadelphia were the cities dearest to Ben Franklin's heart. When he died in 1790, he left each city a thoughtful gift—a donation of £1,000, with an interesting twist: the money was not to be used right away. The fund was to be used to loan between £15 and £60 to young men who had served apprenticeships and were looking to start businesses. A 5 percent interest rate was to be charged, and in this way the fund would grow over the years. Calculating ahead, Franklin predicted that the fund would grow to £131,000 in 100 years. He specified that at this point, £100,000 of that money was to be given to Boston to use for its public works such as roads, bridges, aqueducts, and public buildings. The remaining £31,000 was to continue to serve as a pool of money for loans for another 100 years, after which he estimated the total sum in the fund would be over £4 million. This was to be divided up, with over £1 million going to the City of Boston and the rest to the State of Massachusetts. In 1890, part of the money was released as per Franklin's instructions, but after two Boston aldermen were accused of misusing the funds, a 14-year-long legal dispute ensued over what was to be done with it. In 1990, $4.5 million was left in the Boston fund; it was used to fund the Benjamin Franklin Institute of Technology.

Archaeology in Your Backyard

Archaeologists have discovered much about Boston's historic and prehistoric past through excavations at key locations, including the Boston Common, where Boston's oldest artifact, a 7,500-year-old spear point, was found; Paul Revere's house; and Faneuil Hall. In fact, Boston is known as the "City of Archaeology" because of its hundreds of archaeological sites.

Artifacts have been turning up in and around Boston for many years, both historic (after European settlement) and prehistoric (Native American). Everything from bottles to pottery to bone have turned up in digs around the city. Archaeologists are often called in to check the ground for artifacts when a new building's foundation is being dug, and they have to work quickly to rescue artifacts so that building construction remains on schedule.

In this activity, you will try your hand at an excavation.

ADULT SUPERVISION REQUIRED

YOU'LL NEED

- ★ Tape measure
- ★ 4 long nails (at least 3 inches long) or 12-inch wooden dowels
- ★ Hammer
- ★ String
- ★ Trowels
- ★ Bucket
- ★ Paintbrushes, various sizes
- ★ Pen or pencil
- ★ Notebook
- ★ Camera
- ★ Small Ziploc bags
- ★ Permanent marker
- ★ Flat-bottomed sifter

Find a spot in your backyard or schoolyard where you can dig. Get permission from an adult before digging. Measure out a two-foot-by-two-foot square. Mark each corner by hammering a nail almost all the way into the ground. Then tie string from one nail to the next.

Scrape away at the surface of the ground using the trowel. Remove the loose dirt and place it into a bucket. If you come across an artifact (a piece of glass, bottle cap, coin, etc.), use a paintbrush to clear away the dirt around the object. Write in your notebook the depth at which you found it and photograph it in situ (where it lies). Then carefully remove the object and bag it. Label the bag with the location and date.

As you scrape away the soil, you will notice different colors. This is called stratigraphy, or layering of the soil. Note the depth at which the change occurs and the color of each layer in your notebook. When you reach a new layer, empty the bucket into the sifter and sift the dirt to find small artifact fragments.

Keep digging until you have gone down about one foot. By now you are probably at a level representing the surface hundreds of years ago. When you are done, refill the hole.

funeral, and he was buried in the Granary Burying Ground near the Park Street Church.

Meanwhile, Governor William Dummer issued a warrant for Phillips's arrest for the "barbarous murder" he committed. After the duel, Phillips, who had been only slightly wounded, fled to the house of his brother, Gillam. Gillam's wife was the sister of Peter Faneuil, the builder of Faneuil Hall. To help the killer escape, Faneuil gave him a letter of introduction to his uncle, John Faneuil, who lived in Orleans, France. With help from three other men, Phillips quickly got onto a ship that was sailing for Europe. Phillips landed in Orleans, where he died in exile around 1730.

A month after the duel, a new governor took office and he, along with 87 other prominent Bostonians, signed a petition claiming Phillips was a man of honorable character and asking for his pardon. The letter proclaimed that the signers knew Henry Phillips well and found him to be "very affable, courteous, and peaceable behavior and disposition, and never heard he was addicted to quarreling, he being soberly brought up . . . slow to anger, and with difficulty moved to resentment." The petition did not matter in the end, because Phillips died less than a year after the duel.

Even in the midst of grieving the loss of the young Woodbridge, the official government response to this duel was stern. At the beginning of the General Court's next session on July 24, lawmakers introduced a new law that was intended to prevent dueling. Anyone who engaged in a duel, even if nobody was actually injured, would upon conviction be "carried publicly in a cart to the gallows, with a rope around his neck, and set on the gallows an hour, then to be imprisoned twelve months without bail." Any person killed in a duel was to be denied a Christian burial and be buried with a stake through his body. The survivor of the duel would be buried the same way upon his death.

Smallpox Outbreak

Smallpox was a highly contagious and often deadly disease that ravaged the world during the 18th century. During the peak of the epidemic, as many as 500,000 people died from smallpox in Europe every year. Thanks to ships bearing infected passengers, the disease also affected the New World and plagued Boston. In 1702, 313 Bostonians died during a smallpox outbreak. In 1721, infected sailors who had arrived on a ship from Britain spread a massive epidemic that afflicted half of the city's population and caused 884 smallpox deaths.

One well-known fact about this disease, which caused pus-filled bumps, or pox, all over the body, was that people who had already survived smallpox could not get it again. With this in mind, a new idea to prevent the disease from killing so many people was proposed in Europe during the early 18th century. Called inoculation, this procedure involved penetrating the skin of a healthy person's arm with a small amount of the smallpox virus. To get the virus for the inoculation, a doctor would first scrape the dry scab or the liquid inside the pock of an infected person. This artificially introduced infection would supposedly

A 19th-century cartoon about injecting cowpox virus into humans as prevention for smallpox.

cause a low-grade and less dangerous version of the disease.

Reverend Cotton Mather of Boston was one of the biggest supporters of this method. As the epidemic spread, he took it upon himself to campaign for inoculation. He found a willing doctor named Zabdiel Boylston, who inoculated 244 people. Boylston's method may seem crude now but was sophisticated for the time. He made a couple of incisions into a patient's arm and inserted lint that was dipped in pox liquid. After 24 hours, the lint was removed and the wounds were dressed using cabbage leaves. After seven days, the patient inevitably developed a mild form of smallpox. Those who were inoculated were contagious, so they

had to be quarantined (isolated from other people) until they recovered.

Many Bostonians, including a prominent physician named William Douglass, opposed Mather and Boylston's efforts. They claimed inoculation was dangerous and caused too many people to die.

On November 14, 1721, someone threw a lighted grenade into Reverend Mather's window, with an angry note attached to the fuse. According to Mather, "The Opposition to it has been carried on with senseless Ignorance and raging Wickedness. But the growing Triumphs of Truth over it throw a possessed people into a Fury, which will probably cost me my Life." Of the 287 people inoculated in Boston in 1721, 6 died—a 2.1 percent fatality rate that compared favorably to the 14.6 percent fatality rate in those who contracted the disease naturally.

In 1752, there was another epidemic, again traced to a ship from England bearing infected passengers. This time, Boston officials agreed that inoculation was the right thing to do. The population of Boston at that time was 15,684, and of those 5,545 had already had smallpox and were thus immune, 2,124 were inoculated, and 1,800 fled the city. Thirty of the Bostonians who were inoculated died of the disease, which was just 1.4 percent. A total of more than 500 people died from smallpox that year.

In 1796, an English physician named Edward Jenner discovered that humans infected with cowpox were immune to smallpox without contracting the disease at all. He published his finding in 1798. This news was very exciting, and in 1799 a doctor from Cambridge, Massachusetts, named Benjamin Waterhouse wrote a newspaper article about smallpox vaccination. In 1800, Waterhouse vaccinated two of his sons and one of his servants to demonstrate that vaccination worked. Two years later, the Boston Board of Health did an experiment and vaccinated 22 Bostonians using cowpox. They experienced only the mildest symptoms that cowpox caused in humans. Afterward, these test patients were inoculated with active smallpox virus, and none of the patients showed any sign of smallpox. It worked!

In 1816, a general vaccination took place in Boston, protecting thousands of people from the disease. Between 1811 and 1839, only 52 people died from smallpox. In 1838, an advertisement in the *Boston Medical and Surgical Journal* proclaimed that a person could buy 10 feather quills dipped into smallpox vaccine for one dollar postpaid. In 1855, Massachusetts passed a law that stated all children must be vaccinated against smallpox before the age of two. Smallpox was still a serious issue for Boston, even after the vaccine was available. Between 1839 and 1861, 1,491 Bostonians died from the disease.

Gravestone Designs

Boston and many other cities and towns in the eastern United States have cemeteries dating back to the 17th or 18th centuries. The tops of the earliest surviving gravestones in these cemeteries are often engraved with one of several popular designs of the day, including the winged death's head (literally, a skull with wings), the cherub's head (an angelic child), and the willow and urn. Each design was popular at different times, and in this activity, you will try to figure out the order in which they were popular.

Visit one or more old cemeteries that date back at least to the 18th century. As you walk and explore, make note (or take photos) of the gravestones that feature any of these designs. The key information is the date of death and the type of design. Try to find at least 10 examples of each type of design for this experiment.

When you are done, figure out the date ranges for each design (earliest appearance and latest appearance) as well as the average date (add all the dates for that design together, and then divide by the number of dates). Do you see any patterns emerging? Which design came first and which was the most recent?

Example of a gravestone with a winged death's head. *Author's collection*

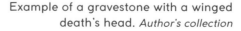

REVOLUTION!

AMERICAN COLONISTS IN the 1760s were unhappy with new laws the British government enacted. One law, the Quartering Act of March 1765, said that Americans had to offer lodging to British officers. Another unpleasant law was the Stamp Act, also passed in March 1765. This law would allow the British to impose taxes on everything from newspapers to playing cards and dice to college degrees. The British government maintained that the taxes were necessary for "defraying the expences of defending, protecting, and securing" the colonies. The citizens

The Boston Tea Party.

of Boston found this, and other acts and events over the next few years, revolting. It was a period of turmoil in Boston, and it would lead to the Revolutionary War.

The Stamp Act

In the spring of 1765, when word arrived in Boston of the Stamp Act, the citizens were outraged. Newspaper publishers instantly opposed the tax because it would affect their business; they would be taxed according to the number of sheets and advertisements their papers contained. In June, the Massachusetts House of Representatives issued a circular to the other colonies suggesting that delegates from each colony meet in in New York in October. This meeting would be known as the Stamp Act Congress. James Otis, Timothy Ruggles, and Oliver Partridge were selected as the Massachusetts representatives, and voters approved a sum of £100 to pay for their journey to New York.

As the summer wore on, Boston citizens became more outraged over the impending taxation, which was to take effect in the fall. On the morning of August 14, 1765, someone hung two effigies, or dummies, from a large elm tree (later known as the Liberty Tree) at the corner of what are now Washington and Essex Streets. One effigy represented Andrew Oliver, who had just been appointed as the stamp distributor for Massachusetts colony. The other was in the form of a boot with a head and devil horns, representing John Stuart, the Earl of Bute, an influential pro-taxation member of the British government. After a few hours, a crowd of people cut down the effigies and carried them along the streets of Boston while yelling, "Liberty and property forever! No stamps! No taxation without our consent!" The crowd marched to a little wooden building that Oliver had erected from which to sell stamps. They tore it down and proceeded to Oliver's house, where they ripped the head off the effigy and broke the house's windows. Next, they took the effigy to Fort Hill and burned it. The crowd then returned to Oliver's house, broke in, threatened to kill him, and started to wreck his furniture and destroy his yard as he escaped out the back door. Scared for his life, he resigned from his job the next day.

Two weeks later another mob ransacked the homes of some government officials, including that of Lieutenant Governor Thomas Hutchinson on North Square. They smashed the front doors with an ax and rushed into the house. Hutchinson and his family had barely escaped just minutes earlier. Within a few hours of arriving, the mob had completely destroyed his house, taking money, furniture, clothes, and silver; wrecking his library; and leaving debris scattered on the street. The angry crowd caused £2,500 worth of damage, a fortune for the time. As Hutchinson's grandson later wrote, based on Hutchinson's own memoirs, "They continued their possession until daylight, destroyed, carried away, or cast into the street, every thing that was in the house; demolished every part of it, except the walls, as far as lay in their power; and had begun to break away the brick-work."

An emergency citizens' meeting the next morning officially condemned the violence in a unanimous vote, though it is likely some of those who voted were part of the mob. After officials posted rewards for the capture of the perpetrators, several suspects were rounded up and thrown in jail to await trial. A small crowd of angry people entered the prison and threatened the prison-keeper until he gave them the keys to the cells. Once they had the keys, they freed all the suspects.

A ship containing stamps arrived in Boston Harbor in September. However, because Oliver had resigned, the stamps went instead to the governor's castle, which the governor ordered guarded with extra men. The governor found himself in a very tricky position. He needed to maintain control and fall in line with the British government, but at the same time seem sympathetic in the eye of the colonists. Not wanting to cause further riots, he proclaimed that though the stamps were in his possession, he had no authority to open the packages or appoint a stamp distributor. In a speech in late September, he proclaimed that although some laws may not be wise or useful, the Parliament had the authority to make laws and it was up to the colonies to follow them. He also said there was a chance the law would be repealed, but only if the colonies first submitted to it.

On November 1, the day the Stamp Act was to take effect, Bostonians heard the eerie sound of muffled bells tolling. The ships in the harbor lowered their flags to half-mast, and effigies of two British politicians hung on the Liberty Tree. One

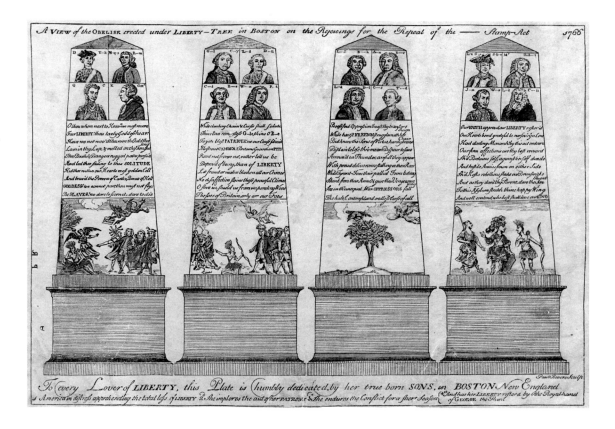

Obelisk erected under the Liberty Tree after the repeal of the Stamp Act in 1766.

effigy represented John Huske, whom the colonists especially hated because he had started out as a merchant in Boston but then moved to Britain and supported taxing the colonies. The effigies had labels on them with angry poems. In the afternoon, colonists cut down the effigies before a crowd of thousands, placed them in a cart, and took them to the gallows at the Neck. After some people gave speeches, the effigies were taken down from the gallows and torn to shreds. The effigies' limbs were tossed into the air. Opposition to the Stamp Act finally led to its repeal in 1766.

Faneuil Hall.

Faneuil Hall

One of Boston's oldest and most famous buildings, Faneuil Hall was built in 1743 at the old town dock. This public meeting hall was the site of many important citizens' meetings, led by the rallying cries of everyone from Samuel Adams to Frederick Douglass. There have been several renovations to this historic building over the years, including in the 1890s, when its wood frame was replaced by steel, and the 1990s, when safety and comfort improvements were made. The only completely original part of the building is the grasshopper weathervane.

Today, Faneuil Hall contains shops, restaurants, and a museum devoted to the Ancient and Honorable Artillery Company of Massachusetts, which was founded in 1638 and has had a home in the building since 1746.

Troops Land in Boston

Even with the repeal of the Stamp Act, there was much discontent in Boston over the continued control Britain exerted over the colonies. A new revenue act effective in October 1767 taxed glass, paint, paper, and tea imported into the colonies. The new taxes led 211 merchants to vow not to import any of the newly taxed items for a year. Others tried to smuggle goods into Boston. When customs officials seized a ship that was attempting to secretly import wine into Boston, the citizens rebelled and attacked the commissioners' houses. A convention called by the people of Boston was held in September 1768, and representatives from 96 towns in Massachusetts—almost every settlement—attended. The convention protested several things, including taxation of the colonies and the idea of an occupying army being sent to Boston.

"Boston is mutinous; its resolves unreasonable and desperate. Mad people procured them; mad people govern the town and the province," wrote General Thomas Gage to his superiors in Britain. Because of its growing unease with the situation in Boston, Britain decided to send armed ships to the city. The ships were loaded with British troops who would be stationed in Boston to keep the order and watch over what Britain felt were unruly and dangerous people. Before long, seven armed ships arrived in Boston to join the one that had already been there. This scene was immortalized in an engraving made by Paul Revere.

A crowd gathered to watch their city being invaded by hundreds of troops. On October 1, 1768, the British 14th, 29th, and 59th Regiments stepped off their ships with guns loaded and bayonets glinting. They marched through the streets, their drums beating out a rhythm and fifes playing, to the Boston Common. The only problem was that housing for the newly arrived troops had not been arranged yet. Some pitched their tents right on the

spot. Others spent the night in Faneuil Hall. There was some disagreement between the British military command and the Common Council over where the troops should be housed. The council proclaimed that although they were required to quarter (or house) the troops, they did not have to do so if there was room for them in the barracks at Castle William, a fort in South Boston. The sheriff tried to take control of an old factory to quarter the troops, but its owners protested with the backing of the Sons of Liberty, a group that was formed to protect colonists' rights, and the sheriff gave up.

Bostonians were dismayed by the situation and reacted accordingly. Soon after the troops arrived, 200 Boston families vowed not to drink any tea, and soon the students of Harvard College agreed

British troops landing in Boston in 1768, engraved by Paul Revere.

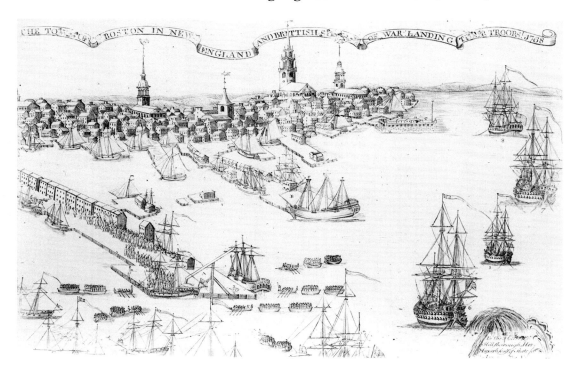

to do the same. The overall mood in the city was desolate. Some of the British officers arranged for a series of dances in Boston that winter to try to lift the veil of gloom over the city and ease the colonists' mistrust of the British army, but none of the women of Boston took the bait. Bostonians resisted this opportunity to be festive because they believed their city to be under a hostile occupation and wanted nothing to do with the soldiers, however gallant they looked in their uniforms.

The Boston Massacre.

As the months passed, tensions remained high. Bostonians looked upon the soldiers as an unwelcome and menacing presence. The British soldiers did nothing to ease that perception. When they set up quarters across from the State House, they placed two cannons outside, pointed at the State House.

In June 1769, the Massachusetts House of Representatives declared that "the establishment of a standing army in the colony, in time of peace, was an invasion of natural rights; that a standing army was not known as a part of the British constitution; and that sending an armed force into the colony under pretence of assisting the civil authority was highly dangerous to the people, unprecedented and unconstitutional."

The British performed random acts of violence and intimidation against the residents of Boston. According to complaints of the time, as summarized in the 19th-century book *The History of Massachusetts: The Provincial Period*, the soldiers "found nothing to do but to insult defenceless females, and parade the streets with clubs in their hands as if provoking a brawl."

The Boston Massacre

By the winter of 1769–70, tensions were at an all-time high. On February 22, 1770, a group of young boys came out into the streets with some mocking pictures they had drawn representing local importers of British goods. A Custom House inspector noticed, tried to grab the pictures, and then yelled at the boys. A crowd of people gathered, and the inspector threatened them. He then walked home. The boys followed him, shouting and then throwing snowballs at his house. He emerged with a gun and shot and killed an 11-year-old boy. Many people attended the boy's funeral and considered him a martyr.

Not long after that, two British soldiers of the 29th Regiment challenged a workman at a ropewalk (a rope-making establishment) to a boxing match. He refused. They returned with reinforcements, about 10 or 12 soldiers, but were beaten back by the ropewalk workmen. They returned once more, this time with 50 soldiers, but were once again made to retreat. The next afternoon, British soldiers returned to the ropewalk and hit some of the workmen. The owner of the ropewalk finally tried to convince them to stand down and avoid further violence, but on March 3, a few soldiers returned with clubs and struck some of the workers.

That week, the city felt the rumblings of more violence to come. On March 1, 1770, a Boston man named William Newhall came across four soldiers who told him that "there were a great many that would eat their dinners on Monday next, that should not eat any on Tuesday." On March 2, the wife of a British soldier named James McDeed heard people in a shop talking about the disturbance at the ropewalk, blaming the soldiers for being aggressive. The woman told them "that before Tuesday or Wednesday night they would wet their swords or bayonets in New England people's blood." On March 4, a soldier named Charles Malone knocked at the door of Amos Thayer's

house and told his sister to pass along a message: "Your brother . . . is a man I have great regard for, and I came on purpose to tell him to keep in his house, for before Tuesday night next at twelve o'clock, there will be a great deal of blood shed, and a great many lives lost." On the morning of March 5, the chatter among the soldiers was especially graphic, and several Bostonians overheard them saying that violence was imminent.

It was true. Though accounts vary in the details, the evening of March 5 was a chaotic and deadly one. Just after 6:00 PM, British soldiers ran through the streets with their swords drawn, yelling at and threatening the people they encountered. One soldier knocked down a 12-year-old boy who was out on an errand. A fight began between about 12 soldiers and a group of young men. The soldiers had a variety of weapons, including swords, clubs, and a shovel.

By about 9:00 PM, a crowd of more than 50 young men armed with sticks gathered around the Custom House, where they taunted a British sentry on duty. The meeting-house bell was ringing, normally a signal for the townspeople to come with buckets to help fight a fire. One of the boys in the crowd insulted the sentry's commanding officer, and the sentry hit him in the head with the butt of his rifle, sending the boy reeling. The crowd began to get rowdier. They threw snowballs and sticks at the sentry. Captain Thomas Preston of the 29th Regiment and eight of his soldiers arrived as backup, and Preston tried to break up the crowd. The snowballs continued to fly and a club was thrown, hitting one of the soldiers.

Crispus Attucks in a 1940s mural.

Witnesses disagree on who yelled what. Some said the people in the crowd were taunting the soldiers to fire. Others claim that Captain Preston yelled "Fire!" Still others said that Preston was telling his men not to fire. What is for certain is that the scene was chaotic and noisy, and at about 9:30 PM one of the soldiers fired his musket and then others followed, killing three people instantly: a young man named Samuel Gray, who worked at the ropewalk; Crispus Attucks, who was half black and half Native American; and James Caldwell. A 17-year-old boy named Samuel Maverick died of his injuries the next morning, and a man named Patrick Carr died eight days later. Six other men were wounded by bullets. Boston was stunned by this tragedy, but the British maintained their innocence in the events of that night.

The funeral for the first four victims was held on March 8. Shops were closed, and the bells of Boston and neighboring towns tolled. A large crowd met the procession of the hearses. The bodies were all buried in the same vault in the burial ground. Patrick Carr was buried with the others on the 17th.

After the massacre, a committee that included Samuel Adams and John Hancock led a massive investigation of the event. They interviewed dozens of eyewitnesses and recorded their testimonies. Several of the soldiers at the scene were put on trial. The commanding officer, Captain Thomas Preston, was acquitted. Two soldiers were found guilty of manslaughter (not murder) and were branded on the hand as punishment.

The Tea Act and the Boston Tea Party

During the 18th century, tea was a much more valuable commodity than it is today. Tea plants grew only in warm climates in distant lands and had to be transported by ship across thousands of miles to get to America. Though earlier taxes from the 1760s had been repealed, England retained a small tax on tea and granted a monopoly for selling tea to the East India Company.

Even though their tax was lower than what British citizens paid for their tea, the colonists rebelled. They refused to buy the tea that was to be taxed. They were angry that they were being taxed without representation. The colonists were also upset about being forced to buy tea through the East India Company. Tea-carrying East India Company ships approaching New York and Philadelphia were not allowed to dock. In Boston, however, the governor prevented the people from sending the newly arrived ships away. Samuel Adams and other patriots argued for the rejection of the tea ships, but the governor held firm. The tea ships arrived under the protection of armed British warships.

After days of tension, on December 16, 1773, over 100 men dressed as Native Americans boarded three ships at what was then known as

The Boston Tea Party.

Griffin's Wharf (now nonexistent because the land was filled in during the 19th century). They dumped 342 crates (45 tons) of precious tea into Boston Harbor, in what became known as the Boston Tea Party. Ironically, the event was planned in a coffeehouse.

One of the participants, George Hewes, remembered years later in his memoirs:

There was a meeting of the citizens of the county of Suffolk, convened at one of the churches in Boston, for the purpose of consulting on what measures might be considered expedient to prevent the landing of the tea, or secure the people from the collection of the duty. At that meeting a committee was appointed to wait on Governor Hutchinson, and request him to inform them whether he would take any measures to satisfy the people on the object of the meeting. To the first application of this committee, the governor told them he would give them a definite answer by five o'clock in the afternoon. At the hour appointed, the committee again repaired to the governor's house, and on inquiry found he had gone to his country seat at Milton, a distance of about six miles. When the committee returned and informed the meeting of the absence of the governor, there was a confused murmur among the members, and the meeting was immediately dissolved, many of them crying out, Let every man do his duty, and be true to his country; and there was a general huzza for Griffin's wharf. It was now evening, and I immediately dressed myself in the costume of an

Indian, equipped with a small hatchet, which I and my associates denominated the tomahawk, with which, and a club, after having painted my face and hands with coal dust in the shop of a blacksmith, I repaired to Griffin's wharf, where the ships lay that contained the tea. When I first appeared in the street, after being thus disguised, I fell in with many who were dressed, equipped and painted as I was, and who fell in with me, and marched in order to the place of our destination.

When the men arrived at the wharf, they were assigned to one of three groups, one group per ship. Hewes was told to fetch the ship's keys from the captain, along with a dozen candles. The captain did not put up a fight and gave the keys to Hewes, asking that no damage be done to his ship.

Said Hewes:

We then were ordered by our commander to open the hatches, and take out all the chests of tea and throw them overboard, and we immediately proceeded to execute his orders; first cutting and splitting the chests with our tomahawks, so as thoroughly to expose them to the effects of the water. In about three hours from the time we went on board, we had thus broken and thrown overboard every tea chest to be found in the ship; while those in the other ships were disposing of the tea in the same way, at the same time. We were surrounded by British armed ships, but no attempt was made to resist us. We then quietly retired to our several places of residence, without having any conversation with each other, or taking any measures to discover who were our associates. . . . There appeared to be an understanding that each individual should volunteer his services, keep his own secret, and risk the consequences for himself.

There were many spectators to this Tea Party, and at least a few decided to try to salvage some of the tea for their own use. Now and then someone would go onto the dock and wait for their chance to "snatch up a handful from the deck, where it became plentifully scattered, and put it into their pockets," according to Hewes. When caught in the act, these tea-grabbers were treated accordingly. A man named O'Conner boarded the ship and when he thought nobody was looking filled his pockets and lining of his coat with tea. He was spotted and he tried to escape, but Hewes grabbed his coat and pulled it from him. As he ran away through the crowd of people on the wharf, they kicked and punched at him as he passed. According to Hewes, "The next day we nailed the skirt of his coat, which I had pulled off, to the whipping post in Charlestown, the place of his residence, with a label upon it, commemorative of the occasion which had thus subjected the proprietor to the popular indignation."

When the next morning Bostonians spotted tea floating on the surface of the water at the wharf, they set out in small boats and pushed down the tea with their oars and paddles to drench it and prevent any of it from being salvageable.

NO TIME TO SELL TEA

This was not a good time to be a tea-seller in Boston, either. One tea-seller named Mrs. Philips had her house smeared with foul-smelling substances. Another tea-seller, a man named Theophilus Lilly, had a sign nailed on a post in front of his house. The sign had a finger pointing to his house painted on it along with the words THAT IS AN IMPORTER OF TEA. One day a German boy named Christopher Seider stood in front of the Lilly residence looking at the sign, and a British customs officer named Ebenezer Richardson insulted him for staring at it. A crowd of people soon gathered in defense of the boy. Richardson retreated to his home, the crowd following him. Richardson went inside and the crowd began yelling at him. He fired his gun through the window, killing the boy. The crowd then broke into Richardson's house, seized him, and brought him into custody. However, Richardson fled to Nova Scotia before a trial could be held.

The Boston Port Act

Though there was no violent retaliation, the British reaction to the Boston Tea Party was an angry one. One member of Parliament, Charles Van, said of the Bostonians, "They ought to have their town knocked about their ears and destroyed." The British government decided to blockade the port of Boston, not allowing any ships in or out until Boston paid for the tea that was destroyed. News of the Boston Port Act arrived on May 10, 1774.

On May 12, Boston invited committees from eight neighboring towns (Dorchester, Roxbury, Brookline, Newton, Cambridge, Charlestown,

Create a Walking Tour of Your Neighborhood

Just as every neighborhood in Boston has a unique history and heritage, so do the neighborhoods in your hometown. Create a special walking tour of your area to help you learn about its rich past. We often get so used to our own neighborhoods that we hardly pay attention to the details. How often do you pass by an old building with a hidden past? A school with a famous alumnus? A church with a secret history? A house that's much older than you think? What interesting facts await discovery about places within walking distance of where you live?

YOU'LL NEED

★ Graph paper

★ 8½-by-11-inch printer paper

★ Pen

★ Computer with internet access

★ Notebook

★ Camera

★ Printer

★ Scanner or copy machine

Using graph paper, map out all or part of your neighborhood—at least a four-block-by-four-block area. Mark each building on the map with a rectangle or appropriate shape. You can use many resources to find information on your neighborhood. If you live in Boston or another large city, look for walking tour and architectural guides. Many cities or counties offer online property searches that yield information about a building (such as the date built or the previous owners' names). You can also check your local library or historical society. They often have old newspaper clippings, maps, photographs, and documents about your neighborhood's history.

After you finish drawing your map, interview longtime neighborhood residents and ask them questions about what the area was like when they moved in. You can also ask if they have any old photographs or stories about certain buildings. Compile the information into a walking tour flyer by numbering the buildings or sites on the map for which you have information. Then pick logical starting and ending points for the tour. For the back or second page of the flyer, write historical facts for each tour stop and perhaps add some digital photos (and maybe scans of old photos, if available).

You can scan the map and create a two-sided flyer, or photocopy it to hand out along with the map legend page. Print out your finished flyer page(s) and you're ready to conduct your tour!

Lynn, and Lexington) to a meeting led by Samuel Adams at Faneuil Hall. The representatives of Boston's neighbors condemned the Boston Port Act as cruel and unjust. The Bostonians knew that its innocent neighbors would suffer from the port of Boston being closed and suggested they pay for the tea, but the eight towns were steadfast and rejected what they believed to be a humiliating offer. They proclaimed they would suffer alongside Boston.

The citizens of Boston met on May 14 and passed a resolution: "That it is of the opinion of this town, that, if the other colonies come to a joint resolution, to stop all importation from Great Britain and the West Indies, till the act, for blocking up this harbor, be repealed, the same will prove the salvation of North American and her liberties. On the other hand, if they continue their exports and imports, there is high reason to fear that fraud, power, and the most odious oppression, will rise triumphant over justice, right, social happiness, and freedom." The Boston government sent copies of the statement to the other colonies, describing the act as "designed to suppress the spirit of liberty in America."

As they received word of what had happened in Boston, citizens throughout the colonies met to take up the cause of New England's biggest city. They set aside June 1, the day the Boston Port Act was to take effect, for fasting and prayer. On June 2, the Boston Committee of Correspondence wrote "A Solemn League and Covenant," whose signers agreed not to buy or consume any goods from Great Britain. Governor Thomas Gage called

the resolution illegal and traitorous and vowed to have anyone who signed it arrested.

But it was too late. The outrage over the closing of Boston's port was spreading through the colonies, and the colonists were voicing their support and protest. They were forming a united front that would lead to the first Continental Congress meeting in September 1774 to show support for Boston and proclaim the colonies' right to self-government.

The Siege of Boston and Bunker Hill

On the night of April 18, 1775, British troops marched from Boston toward Concord to seize American weapons. Paul Revere was one of the riders who set off that night to warn that the "redcoats" were coming. An army of Massachusetts militiamen met the British troops at Lexington, and the scrappy Americans forced the well-trained British into a retreat on April 19. The Revolutionary War had begun.

Feeling confident after this victory, the Americans decided it would be easy to lay siege to British-occupied Boston because of its location on a peninsula. Starting on April 19, 1775, they made their move to cut off Boston from the rest of the mainland. Though they had inferior manpower and firepower, the Americans worked hard to intimidate the British stationed in Boston.

In May 1775, American general John Thomas repeatedly marched his 700 troops around a hill that was visible from Boston so that it looked like he had more soldiers than he did. It worked; the

British thought the force was 2,000 or 3,000 strong. The Americans also marched 2,200 troops 1½ miles from Cambridge to Charlestown, a stone's throw from Boston, and then back to Cambridge. This move was meant to both intimidate the British and inspire confidence in the Americans.

On May 21, with feed for their horses quickly running out, the British military command sent a party of men to Grape Island, about six miles southeast of Boston, which was well stocked with cattle, sheep, and hay. The Americans found out and began firing on the British, who left with three tons of hay. The Americans took a boat to Grape

Island and set fire to the rest of the hay, 80 tons' worth. They systematically took other islands nearby, burned the hay, and removed the livestock before the British could get to them.

The situation in Boston was growing dire. Anyone who deposited their arms at Faneuil Hall was allowed to leave Boston with their personal possessions. The story changed from day to day. According to Abigail Adams, "There are but very few who are permitted to come out in a day . . . one day, they shall come out with their effects; the next day, merchandise is not effects. One day, their household furniture is to come out; the next, only wearing apparel."

The response was staggering; people wishing to flee the city dropped off 2,412 guns and 973 bayonets on April 27 alone. By early June, the only people who remained were the extremely poor, who had no place to go or no way to support themselves if they left. During the siege, some who supported the British (known as Tories) also fled to Boston, figuring they were safer there than in the surrounding countryside.

On May 25, a ship carrying three British major generals (William Howe, John Burgoyne, and Henry Clinton) arrived at Boston. General Burgoyne expressed disbelief at the situation: "What! Ten thousand peasants keep five thousand king's troops shut up! Well, let us get in, and we'll soon find elbow-room!"

On June 15, 1775, the Americans found out that the British planned to occupy Dorchester Heights and the Charlestown peninsula near Boston, which would give them a strategic advantage

The Death of General Warren at the Battle of Bunker's Hill, 17 June, 1775, a print of the famous painting by John Trumbull.

over the entire area. American general Artemis Ward, desperate to keep the British from fulfilling their plans, ordered 1,000 troops under Colonel William Prescott to fortify the Charlestown hills. On the night of June 16, these 1,000 Massachusetts and Connecticut men spent 12 exhausting hours building a fortification. Though Bunker Hill was higher, Breed's Hill was in a better position, so they focused their efforts there. British ships spotted the Americans and opened fire on them, but this did not stop the patriots from doing their work.

Major General Howe addressed his officers on the morning of June 17, telling them, "If the enemy will not come from their intrenchments, we must drive them out at all events, otherwise the town of Boston will be set on Fire by them."

The Battle of Bunker Hill took place at 3:00 PM as 2,000 British troops advanced on the Americans, who opened fire only when the British were at close range. The Americans released a barrage of blinding gunfire from well-protected positions, and the British were decimated and shaken. They retreated, regrouped, and attacked again but soon retreated again. Bolstered by additional troops, the British rallied once more and charged a third time. This third effort proved to be too much for the Americans, who were now short on ammunition. By 5:00 PM, the British overpowered and overran the Americans, forcing them to retreat to Cambridge. The British lost 226 men (with 828 injured) and the Americans 140 men (with 271 injured), but the British had won the battle. Now the British were in control of the Charlestown peninsula.

PLAY MEETS REALITY

Despite the hard times, the British put on plays to amuse themselves. One such play, a farce called *The Siege of Boston*, was about to start on the night of January 8, 1776. When the man playing General George Washington came onto the stage with a long wig and rusty sword, an actual British officer rushed onto the stage and shouted, "The Yankees are attacking Bunker Hill!" Though at first the audience assumed it was part of the play, they soon realized that it was no fiction. The Americans under General Knowlton did lead a raid into British-occupied Charlestown, burning the houses, killing one person, and taking five prisoners.

The Americans' greatest loss was General Joseph Warren, who was president of the Massachusetts Provincial Congress. His death is commemorated in a famous painting by John Trumbull.

Meanwhile, back in Boston, the tension continued. During the summer of 1775, the British chopped down the Liberty Tree. The British removed the best pew in the Old South Church and brought it to the home of a loyalist named John Amory to use as a pigsty. Other churches were used to house soldiers or as timber and fuel.

The winter of 1775–76 was rough for Boston. Diseases such as smallpox were rampant, and food was in short supply. According to Lord Dartmouth, the British were "cooped up in a town, deprived of the comforts and necessaries of life, wasting away by disease and desertion faster than we can recruit, liable to surprise, and no longer the object of terror to the rebels." Now, the British

Walk the Freedom Trail

Boston's Freedom Trail is a 2½-mile-long route that passes 16 historic 18th- and 19th-century sites. As you walk the route, you will see sites such as the Boston Common, Massachusetts State House, Park Street Church, Granary Burying Ground, King's Chapel, King's Chapel Burying Ground, Benjamin Franklin statue and Boston Latin School, Old Corner Bookstore, Old South Meeting House, Old State House, site of the Boston Massacre, Faneuil Hall, Paul Revere House, Old North Church, Copp's Hill Burying Ground, Bunker Hill monument, and the USS *Constitution*. You can find a map of the trail and more information on each of the stops at www.thefreedomtrail .org.

As you walk, take photos of each historic site so you can make your own scrapbook of Boston's history.

had no interest in keeping Bostonians in the city; they were just extra trouble. Besides, their abandoned houses could be used for firewood. Over the winter, Major General Howe had 1,000 Boston residents shipped out of town and landed at points along the harbor.

The British Evacuate Boston

While the British were struggling in Boston, hundreds of miles away, American colonel Henry Knox was leading a successful operation to transport 60 tons of captured heavy artillery from Fort Ticonderoga, New York, to Boston. General George Washington had these cannons placed in nearby Cambridge and Roxbury, and on March 2 the Americans opened fire on Boston. General Howe wanted to attack, but a snowstorm prevented him from doing so. He decided instead to give up Boston. On March 17, 1776, the British made a mass exit from the city. All told, 120 ships carrying 11,000 people, mostly British troops, departed Boston Harbor.

By this point, the Declaration of Independence had not even been written and the war had barely begun, but Boston was safe. It was now back in American hands, where it would remain for the next seven long years of America's struggle for independence. Boston would serve as a bastion for freedom and a source of much-needed supplies.

One If by Land

Paul Revere had been . . . well . . . a revered name in Boston history since the late 18th century when the talented artist and silversmith made a lasting mark for himself as a dedicated patriot and member of the Sons of Liberty. But his true place in American folklore was not sealed until 1860, when the Boston poet Henry Wadsworth Longfellow published a poem called "Paul Revere's Ride." In the beginning of the poem, Longfellow writes:

Listen, my children, and you shall hear
Of the midnight ride of Paul Revere,

On the eighteenth of April, in Seventy-Five:
Hardly a man is now alive
Who remembers that famous day and year.
He said to his friend, "If the British march
By land or sea from the town to-night,
Hang a lantern aloft in the belfry-arch
Of the North-Church-tower as a signal light,—
One if by land, and two if by sea"

Thus begins Revere's adventure, and his legend. Revere's ride was well known even before the poem was written, but did the famous "one if by land" moment actually happen? It sure did, according to Revere's own words as he recounted the events years later in a letter to the Massachusetts Historical Society: "I returned at night through Charlestown; there I agreed with a Colonel Conant and some other gentlemen, that if the British went out by water, we would show two lanterns in the North Church steeple; and if by land, one, as a signal, for we were apprehensive it would be difficult to cross the Charles River, or get over Boston Neck."

Samuel Adams

Boston played a critical role in the battle for freedom from Great Britain, and Samuel Adams was one of its most important leaders in that fight. Born in 1722, Adams (second cousin of John Adams, future president) graduated from Harvard in 1740. His father, a brewer, entered politics in 1746 as a Representative of Boston. Upon the elder Adams's death in 1748, Samuel took over the brewery, but

The Paul Revere House in Boston.

Paul Revere.

this was not his sole ambition in life; in fact, his business did not thrive. He began to contribute to newspapers, writing pieces defending colonists' rights. By 1764, he had become one of the most vocal critics of British rule, drafting a document against parliamentary taxation. He entered the Massachusetts legislature in 1765 (a position in which he remained until 1774) and was one of the organizers of the Sons of Liberty, a powerful patriotic group that arose in protest of the Stamp Act.

In the years that followed, he was a tireless writer, penning piece after piece championing the rights of the colonies and protesting taxation and British rule in general. His words inspired Bostonians to protest and revolt. He was a Massachusetts delegate to the Continental Congress from 1774 to 1781, where he served on many committees and continued to be a powerful voice for independence.

In 1775, together with his cousin John, Samuel Adams nominated George Washington to be commander in chief of the army. Adams, a signer of the Declaration of Independence, was one of the first leaders to call for the colonies to break away from Great Britain.

As an eloquent orator and writer, Samuel Adams was adept at using words to lead the colonies toward freedom. At a meeting where the difficulties of the struggle against Britain were being discussed, he said:

Samuel Adams.

A Grecian philosopher who was lying asleep upon the grass, was aroused by the bite of some animal upon the palm of his hand. He closed his hand suddenly as he woke and found that he had caught a field mouse. As he was examining the little animal who dared to attack him, it unexpectedly bit him a second time, and made its escape. Now, fellow citizens what think you was the reflection he made upon this trifling

Boston in 1778.

circumstance? It was this: that there is no ani-mal, however weak and contemptible, which cannot defend its own liberty, if it will only fight for it.

After the war, Samuel Adams became lieuten-ant governor and then governor of Massachusetts before retiring from public life in 1797. He died in 1803.

Make a Liberty Broadside

In the 18th century, there were no telephones, radios, televisions, or computers. The only way for people to communicate in the moment was in person or through newspapers, flyers, or posters. During times of turmoil, newspapers gave people a way to express their opinions. The following British political cartoon from the 1770s shows Bostonians held captive in a cage that is suspended from the Liberty Tree. Three British sailors standing in a boat are feeding them fish from a basket labeled "To — from the Committee of —" in return for a bundle of papers labeled "Promises." Around the tree and in the background are cannons and British troops. While newspapers were good sources of opinions and information, the best way to inform the public about something was by printing a broadside. Broadsides were large, one-sided papers that featured important announcement or proclamations. They might be posted around town or read at a public meeting. They were sometimes sold, depending on the content.

YOU'LL NEED

★ 8½-by-11-inch or 11-by-17-inch printer paper

★ Computer with word-processing software

★ Printer

A British political cartoon from 1774.

Imagine it is 1767 and you live in Boston. You have just formed a new society called the Boston Free Thinkers. The goal of your group is to get people to think about the political situation and figure out ways to unite Boston citizens against British oppression. The purpose of your broadside is both to inform the public about your group and to tell them when and where the group's next meeting will be held. The catch is that since this broadside will be posted in public, its wording has to be cautious and clever. You do not want the British authorities or anyone sympathizing with them to report you.

A T a Meeting of the Freeholders and other Inhabitants of the *Town* of BOSTON, legally qualified and warned, in Publick Town-Meeting, affembled at Faneuil-Hall on Monday the 21ft Day of *April*, Anno Domini, 1766.

VOTED, That the Selectmen be defir'd, when they fhall have a certain Account of the Repeal of the Stamp-Act, to notify the Inhabitants of the Time they fhall fix upon for the general Rejoicings, and to publifh the following Vote, viz.

" UNDER the deepeft Senfe of Duty and Loyalty to our Moft Gracious SOVEREIGN King GEORGE, and in Refpect and Gratitude to the prefent Patriotic Miniftry, Mr. PITT, and the glorious Majority of both Houfes of Parliament, by whofe Influence, underDivine Providence, againft a moft ftrenuous Oppofition, a happy Repeal of the Stamp-Act, fo unconftitutional as well as grievous to His Majefty's good Subjects of AMERICA, is attained ; whereby our inconteftibleRight of InternalTaxation ftill remains tousinviolate :

" VOTED, That at the Time the Selectmen fhall appoint, every Inhabitant be defired to illuminate his Dwelling-Houfe ; and that it is the Senfe of the Town, that the Houfes of the Poor, as well as thofe where there are fick Perfons, and all fuch Parts of Houfes as are ufed for Stores, together with the Houfes of thofe (if there are any) who from certain religious Scruples cannot conform to this Vote, ought to be protected from all Injury ; and that all Abufes and Diforders on the Evening for Rejoicing, by breaking Windows or otherwife, if any fhould happen, be profecuted by the Town.

A true Copy, Atteft. WILLIAM COOPER, *Town-Clerk.*

T HE Selectmen *having received certain Intelligence, that the Act repealing the* Stamp-Act, *has paffed all the requifite Formalities, congratulate the Inhabitants of the Town on the joyful News, and appoint Monday next, the* 19th *Inftant, for the Day of General Rejoicing, in Compliance with the foregoing Votes, recommending to all Perfons a due and punctual Obfervance of the falutary Regulations enjoined therein.*

By Order of the Selectmen,

William Cooper, *Town-Clerk.*

Bofton, May 16. 1766.

One example: THE BOSTON FREE THINKERS ARE DEDICATED TO THE PURSUIT OF ALL THAT IS FAIR AND RIGHT FOR ALL BOSTONIANS. WE SEEK AN OPEN DIALOGUE ON THE CURRENT SITUATION SO AS TO HELP EXAMINE ALL SIDES OF THE PRESENT MOMENT.

Using word-processing software, experiment with large (24 points or greater), easily readable fonts and make your broadside fill the entire sheet of paper. Use a border around the entire page to attract attention.

A Boston broadside from 1766 regarding the repeal of the Stamp Act.

4

FEDERAL CITY

BOSTON CONTINUED TO grow and change in the decades following the end of the Revolutionary War, and it was a very important part of the new republic. The massive Beacon Hill was leveled, and a new State House was built. Boston was a busy port city, with numerous wharves and ships that traveled around the world, bringing back exotic goods from places as far away as China. As immigrants began to pour in from Ireland, the city changed from predominantly English Protestant to Irish Catholic.

The New State House. *Wikimedia Commons/NYPL*

Too Far North

During the Revolutionary War, the Continental Congress met in several different locations, for reasons including safety. After the war ended, there was much discussion within the young republic as to where the federal government should be permanently located. All in all, 24 different locations were proposed for the capital between 1783 and 1789!

Though it was one of the largest and most important cities in the infant nation, leaders did not seriously consider Boston for the honor because it was simply too far north and a more centrally located city was more desirable. Even New York was considered too far north. Ultimately, another factor played into the decision—the capital should be a new creation and not an existing city. Finally, on July 9, 1790, the House of Representatives passed an act "for establishing the temporary and permanent seat of government" on the banks of the Potomac River in Virginia, by the narrow margin of 32–29.

How did the Massachusetts delegation feel about the bill? Not very enthusiastic. All eight members of the Massachusetts delegation to the House of Representatives voted no, as did all the representatives from New Hampshire, Connecticut, and New York. President Washington approved the bill on July 16, and thus ended the seven-year-long struggle.

The Leveling of Beacon Hill

Hills have survived development in few modern American cities (San Francisco, for example). In most cases, hills were leveled to make development easier and transportation more convenient. This was what happened in Boston, which was once known for its three prominent hills: Copp's Hill, Fort Hill, and Beacon Hill.

During the 18th century, people began to dig up the earth on the sides of Beacon Hill and cart it away for use in creating docks and wharves. In 1764, a man named Thomas Hodson, who lived

The leveling of Beacon Hill took place over a 50-year period starting in the 1760s.

on the north side of the hill, was digging up gravel on his property along the slope of the hill and thus threatening its stability. The city tried to buy his land to stop the damage, but Hodson refused to sell or to stop digging.

Despite this, the hill continued to stand. Its height and position meant that it offered spectacular views. In 1792, a visitor named Nathaniel Cutting wrote, "From the summit [of Beacon Hill] one may behold the most variegated and luxuriant scenery that nature and art combined present through her extensive works." Yet the excavation of the hill continued as the years passed. Henry K. Oliver, who used to fly his kite on Beacon Hill as a boy, recalled the man who supervised the excavation in 1808–9 and "how savagely we boys regarded him as the destroyer of our hill of fun and look out."

In 1811, the City of Boston, which owned the summit of the hill, sold it at auction to raise money. The new owners immediately began leveling it, spelling the end for the hill. The dirt excavated from Beacon Hill was used to fill in Mill Pond. The famous Bulfinch-designed monument was removed, and the hill was leveled. Once 138 feet above sea level, the hill was reduced by 60 feet. An 1811 lithograph shows the dramatic sight of the hill being excavated. It did not take long to complete this work. An 1818 book, *A Topographical and Historical Description of Boston*, described Beacon Hill as "now levelled to its base," part of neighboring Copp's Hill taken down, and the summit of Fort Hill leveled.

Make a Time Capsule

In the 18th and 19th centuries, people commonly buried time capsules under a building's foundation or in boxes planted into the building's cornerstone during construction. For example, the Massachusetts State House in Boston contained a time capsule that Paul Revere and Samuel Adams buried in 1795. Workers unearthed the cornerstone capsule in 2014 when work was being done to fix a leak. They slowly and carefully removed, X-rayed, and then eventually opened the copper box. Inside were 23 coins, including a rare and valuable "pine tree shilling" from 1652, a copper medal depicting George Washington, some newspapers, and a silver plate (believed to have been engraved by Paul Revere) that commemorated the dedication of the State House in 1795. Many other important buildings around the country contain cornerstone time capsules, including the Washington Monument.

In this activity, you will create your own cornerstone time capsule.

YOU'LL NEED

* ★ Variety of small everyday items
* ★ Box (cardboard, wood, or metal), at least 6 inches high by 12 inches long and 2 inches deep, with a cover

Imagine that you are in charge of filling a small box to be placed in the cornerstone of a new building in Boston. What items would you put in it? How would they differ from the items you would put into a box to be buried in your own yard or local park?

Choose a variety of everyday items that represent different aspects of life and of the country today. You could enclose newspaper or magazine articles, photos you've taken, coins or paper money, and a letter you write to someone in the future.

If you're doing this with friends or classmates, exchange boxes when you're done. Whose box do you think gives the most complete and interesting picture of modern life in America?

A Tale of Two State Houses

The city's original government building, the Boston Town House (later known as the Old State House) was built on the corner of King Street (now State Street) and Cornhill Street (now Washington Street) in 1657 and destroyed by fire in 1711. Its replacement, constructed in 1712–13, was damaged by fire in 1747 and reconstructed the next year.

Originally a center for the colonial government under British rule, the Old State House played a central role in the country's early days. Many an important discussion took place under its roof during the time leading up to the Revolution. It was from the balcony that Colonel Thomas Crafts read the Declaration of Independence to Boston's citizens on July 18, 1776. The Old State House was also home to the Massachusetts Supreme Judicial Court.

As important and historic as the building was, it was too small to suit the needs of a growing city and state. The government needed a new and larger building. Leaders selected a site on Beacon Hill on what was once John Hancock's pasture land, facing the Boston Common. (The original Hancock House stood nearby until it was demolished in 1863.) Charles Bulfinch designed the New State House, and its cornerstone was laid on July 4, 1795. It was carried to the site on a cart decorated with ribbons and drawn by 15 white horses. Governor Samuel Adams laid the stone with assistance from Paul Revere and other members of the Grand Lodge of Masons. The men placed under the stone a silver plate engraved with the names

The Old State House.

of those laying the stone as well as a handful of coins. In January 1798, the General Court made a procession from the Old State House to the New State House.

The new building was originally 173 feet long and 61 feet deep, and cost $133,333 to build. The 53-foot-diameter, 35-foot-high dome was originally whitewashed wood, but Paul Revere covered it with copper in 1802. After that it was painted gray, and later gold. In 1831, fireproof rooms were added to the building. In 1874, workers layered the dome in 23-karat gold leaf.

By 1888, the population of Massachusetts was increasing, and it was clear that more room was needed for the proper functioning of the state government. The government bought homes behind the building and had them demolished, along with parts of several streets, to make way for the 400-foot-long annex, which was completed in 1895. Another major expansion happened from

Draw Your Own Federal-Style Mansion

The Federal style of architecture was the first distinctly American style. Popular between 1780 and 1830, it built upon the features of the Georgian style, an English import that had been popular earlier in the 18th century. The Federal style kept the classical symmetry of Georgian architecture but was lighter, was less formal, and had more intricate details.

The name most associated with the Federal style is Boston architect Charles Bulfinch (1763–1844). After having spent some time in London after the Revolution, Bulfinch returned to Boston and designed his first building, the Hollis Street Church, in 1787. Other Federal-style masterpieces followed, and before long his services were in high demand in Boston. But Bulfinch's work was not confined to Boston; he was also the third architect of the US Capitol Building, 1818–1829.

Thanks in large part to Bulfinch, the Federal style became popular across the East Coast, but many of the best remaining examples are in and around Boston, including the Massachusetts State House and New North Church (both Bulfinch designs), and 55 Beacon Street.

YOU'LL NEED

* ★ Computer with internet access
* ★ Graph paper
* ★ Pencils (black and a selection of colors including red for the brick)
* ★ Ruler

Look at the photograph of the State House on page 59, and look up other Federal-style buildings in Boston. What do they have in common? See if you can come up with a mansion of your own design, using elements and themes from the buildings you see. Note the symmetry; the classical features; the look of the windows, doors, and roof; and the overall shape of the building. Draw your mansion to a scale of 1 inch equals 10 feet.

1914 to 1918, when a neighboring street and its houses were removed to make room for the new east and west wings of the State House. During World War II, the dome was painted black to protect it from becoming an obvious nighttime bombing target.

Some years after the state government transferred to the new building, the Old State House was used as a City Hall (1830–1841) and later as a commercial building that was home to the United States Telegraph Company, North American Fire Insurance Company, and Reed & Brother Fire & Life Insurance. But toward the end of the 19th century, the building was in danger of being lost. The Bostonian Society, formed in 1881, took over the historic building and made sure it was preserved. Today, the Old State House, Boston's oldest public building, houses a museum that highlights its key role in the city, state, and nation's history. The current State House still functions as the Massachusetts government center.

Boston Goes to China

Boston's strategic location on the Atlantic Ocean made it one of the most important port cities in North America from the first years of its existence as a British colony. The Boston waterfront was alive with the sounds, sights, and smells of a busy seaport. Shipbuilding was one of the biggest Boston industries—in 1743 alone, 30 ships were built in Boston shipyards.

Free of British rule after the Revolution, the port of Boston continued to thrive. Newly built, sturdy ships set sail for ports all across the world, and many from distant lands arrived. In 1790, 455 vessels of all sizes came to Boston. By 1794, Boston had 80 wharves and quays, the largest of which was Long Wharf, which extended over 1,700 feet into the harbor.

Boston's merchants recognized the lucrative potential of trade with the Far East and in the late 1780s began to send ships to China seeking teas, silk, cotton, sugar, coffee, and spices. These China-bound ships generally stopped in the Pacific Northwest on the way to China to load up on furs for trade. The ship *Margaret*, which sailed to the Northwest from Boston in 1791, collected 1,500 otter skins and sold them for $30 to $40 each in China, for great profit. So common were Boston ships on the Northwest coast that Native Americans there called the people they saw "Boston men."

Some of the voyages to the Far East were quite historic. The Boston ship *Columbia*, which sailed for China via Cape Horn in 1787 and returned to Boston in 1790, became the first American ship to circumnavigate the globe.

Other important expeditions to China followed, including the voyage of the ship *Hope*, captained by Joseph Ingraham. He set sail in September 1790 and reached Cape Horn in January 1791. In April 1792, on his way north in the Pacific as he passed through the Marquesas Islands, he made an important discovery when he sighted seven uncharted islands. After checking his maps to be sure, he wrote in his journal that it was "a day ever memorable to Americans." He named

Long Wharf today.

Boston in 1841.

Make a Nautical Chart

Just as maps show the contours of the surface (topography), sea charts show the contours of the sea floor, or underwater topography. This information is extremely useful to anyone who is trying to navigate a boat. Through the ages, countless shipwrecks have been caused by underwater reefs, shoals, and rocks. Boston Harbor is dotted with islands, making navigation especially tricky. In this activity, you'll make a small pond and then create a nautical chart for it.

ADULT SUPERVISION REQUIRED

YOU'LL NEED

- ★ Shovel
- ★ Handful of rocks, various sizes
- ★ Bucket(s) of water
- ★ 4 dowels, about 12 inches long each
- ★ Yardstick (or tape measure) and 2 12-inch rulers
- ★ String, at least 50 feet
- ★ Scissors
- ★ 45/45/90 drafting triangle or square piece of cardboard
- ★ Graph paper
- ★ Pencil
- ★ Calculator

1. With an adult's help, find a place outside where you can dig a hole in the ground, about 1 foot long by 8 inches wide. Vary the depth of the hole. For example, you can make it shallow (2 inches) around the edges, but deeper (at least 6 inches) toward the center. Or you could make it mostly shallow with a few deep trenches in spots. When you are done digging, pat the bottom of the hole with your palms to compact the dirt as much as possible. (If you cannot dig outside, you can try this activity indoors, on a smaller scale, using a large plastic storage container filled with dirt.)

2. Put the two largest rocks aside. Scatter the other rocks in the hole, especially in the shallow areas.

3. Get a bucket (or buckets) of water and very slowly fill the hole. The sides may erode a little as you pour, but that's OK. Stop when the water is about ½ inch or so from the ground surface.

4. Next, you will make a grid so you can take and record depth measurements on your chart. First, place a dowel into the ground near each corner of the pond. Position them so the distance between the far dowels is 14 inches and the distance between the near dowels 12 inches.

5. Tie a string from one dowel to the next at about 6 inches above the ground level and use the drafting triangle to make sure you have a perfect rectangle (adjusting the dowels if necessary).

6. Your chart's scale will be 1:2, so on the graph paper, draw a rectangle that is 7 inches by 6 inches.

7. Cut seven pieces of string that are 18 inches long, and five pieces of string that are 22 inches long. Tie the pieces of string to the dowels from one side of the rectangle to the other at 1-inch intervals, so when you are done you have a grid of strings as shown.

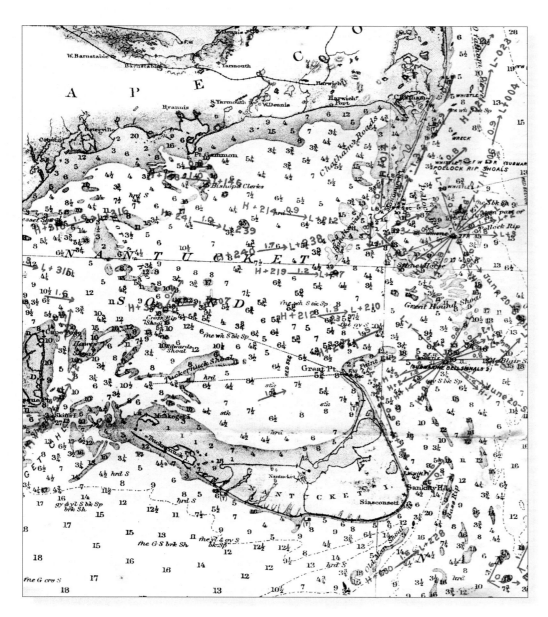

A 19th-century nautical chart of Boston Harbor. *Author's collection*

8. Lightly duplicate this grid on your graph paper. Since your scale is 1:2, the grid lines should be 1 inch apart on the paper.

9. At each of the intersections of the grid that fall above the pond, use the ruler to measure the depth down to the nearest 1/16 of an inch. Use a calculator to figure out the decimal value. (Example: $^{43}/_{16}$ = 4.18 inches)

10. Record each depth number at the correct point on your chart.

the first Washington's Island "in honour to the illustrious president of the United States of America." The others he called Adams's Island, Federal Island, Lincoln's Island, Franklin's Island, Hancock's Island, and Knox's Island (after political and military leaders of the day).

The *Columbia* sailed again from Boston in September 1790 under Captain Robert Gray and landed in the Pacific Northwest in June 1791. Captain Gray explored the coast and in the spring of 1792 discovered the Columbia River. He sailed 24 miles along the river and laid claim to the land that was to become part of the Oregon Territory.

Irish Boston

Boston is very much an Irish city, and today embraces and celebrates its Irish heritage. But in the early days of Boston's settlement, people looked upon the Irish with disdain and suspicion. Early Boston was largely made up of people of English descent, and the English and Irish were historically not the best of friends.

In the decades after Boston was settled, a number of Irish families lived among the mainly English settlers. The city's early birth and marriage records show distinctly Irish names such as Healy, Kelly, Kenny, McCarty, McCue, and Mulligan. Many of these early Irish immigrants were sold into servitude to pay for their ship's passage. Most of the early Irish were, like their English counterparts, Protestants. In 1687, there were only about five Irish Catholics in all of Boston. Despite the relatively few Irish in Boston at the time, anti-Irish feelings were clearly present. In 1700, Reverend Cotton Mather spoke of a plot to send a "Colony of Irish" to Boston "to check the growth of this Countrey."

Though more Irish arrived over the second half of the 17th century, it was not until the 18th century that they began to come to Boston by the hundreds. The first ship of Irish immigrants arrived in 1717. In 1720, the colony's General Court resolved, "Whereas, it appears that certain families recently arrived from Ireland, and others from this province, have presumed to make a settlement . . . that the said people be warned to move off within the space of seven months, and if they fail to do so, that they be prosecuted by the attorney general, by writs of trespass and ejectment." Nothing was done, but at a town meeting in 1723, leaders passed an order that said anyone who arrived in the last three years from Ireland, and anyone who arrives in the future, must go to the Town Clerk and register their names and occupations within five days, or pay a fine of 20 shillings. It also said anyone lodging Irish arrivals had to register with the Town Clerk within 48 hours or pay a 20-shilling fine.

The ships kept coming. Between 1736 and 1738, 10 ships sailed from Ireland to Boston, with a total of almost 1,000 passengers on board. So many Irish were in Boston by this time (many of them poor) that in 1737, they formed a charity called the Irish Society. Its mission was "affectionate and compassionate concern for their countrymen in

Write a Poem in the Style of Ralph Waldo Emerson

Born in Boston in 1803, Ralph Waldo Emerson was educated at the Boston Latin School and then Harvard Divinity School. Originally ordained as a minister, he gave up the clergy after the death of his wife and joined the American transcendentalist movement in the 1830s. The transcendentalists believed that people could go beyond the physical world by being in touch with their spiritual side. Emerson began to lecture and write poems and essays. He also founded a literary magazine. His works look at nature as its own miracle, unrestricted by the chains of religion, its meaning to be found within itself.

Read the two poems below and then see if you can write a short poem about nature in the style of Emerson.

Earth-Song

"Mine and yours;
Mine, not yours.
Earth endures;
Stars abide—
Shine down in the old sea;
Old are the shores;
But where are old men?
I who have seen much,
Such have I never seen.

"The lawyer's deed
Ran sure,
In tail,
To them, and to their heirs
Who shall succeed,
Without fail,
Forevermore.

"Here is the land,
Shaggy with wood,

With its old valley,
Mound and flood.
But the heritors? —
Fled like the flood's foam.
The lawyer, and the laws,
And the kingdom,
Clean swept herefrom.

"They called me theirs,
Who so controlled me;
Yet every one
Wished to stay, and is gone,
How am I theirs,
If they cannot hold me,
But I hold them?"

When I heard the Earth-song
I was no longer brave;
My avarice cooled
Like lust in the chill of the grave.

Fable

The mountain and the squirrel
Had a quarrel,
And the former called the latter 'Little Prig.'
Bun replied,
'You are doubtless very big;
But all sorts of things and weather
Must be taken in together,
To make up a year
And a sphere.
And I think it no disgrace
To occupy my place.
If I'm not so large as you,
You are not so small as I,
And not half so spry.
I'll not deny you make
A very pretty squirrel track;
Talents differ; all is well and wisely put;
If I cannot carry forests on my back,
Neither can you crack a nut.'

these parts, who may be reduced by sickness, shipwreck, old age, and other infirmities and unforeseen accidents."

Eighteenth-century voyages were long and dangerous. As ships were powered only by the wind, the trip could take weeks. One tragic voyage was that of the *Seaflower*, which set sail for Boston from Belfast, Ireland, on July 10, 1740, with 106 passengers. It was plagued by many troubles. The voyage wound up lasting 16 weeks. Starvation and disease were rampant, and the survivors were forced to resort to cannibalism until they spotted a British warship, which rescued them and brought them to Boston. Forty of the passengers and all the crew members had died by the time the ship finally arrived on October 31. The 65 people who survived were in a terribly weak state and were taken to the hospital on Rainsford Island (a quarantine site in Boston Harbor about three miles from the city) to recover.

Poor and overcrowded ship conditions led the General Court to pass a law in 1750 that said no captain could import to Massachusetts "any greater number of passengers in any one Ship or other Vessel than such only as shall be provided with good and wholesome Meat, Drink, and other Necessaries for Passengers." It also said that everyone over the age of 14 had to have a space on the ship that was at least 6 feet long and 1½ feet wide. Violators were to be charged a fine of five pounds per passenger.

Many Boston-area Irishmen served fearlessly at the Battles of Concord, Lexington, and Bunker Hill during the early days of the Revolutionary War. Hugh Cargill, born in Ballyshannon, Ireland, served as a sergeant at Bunker Hill and also rescued the Concord town records during the battle there.

Despite Irish contributions to the birth of the new nation, anti-Irish sentiment continued to rear its head over the next century. Still, there were moments of great pride, such as in 1833, when members of the Irish Society visited with President Andrew Jackson (whose parents were from Ireland) while he was in Boston. Yet in 1834, a Boston government report said that "Foreigners are arriving in great numbers. . . . They find intoxicating liquors in kind profusion and cheapness. . . . They get crazy drunk, and disturb the public peace. . . . These foreigners are principally Irish."

By the mid-19th century, the potato famine in Ireland caused thousands more Irish to immigrate to Boston. In 1850, the city's population was 138,788, of which 52,923, or 38 percent, were Irish born. Boston was rapidly becoming an Irish city.

By 1870, Irish immigrants made up 65 percent of all the foreign-born people in Boston. The Philo-Celtic Society was formed in 1873 to promote the study of the Irish language and republish books in Irish. The society even founded a school open to anyone who wished to study the Irish language.

Boston Museums

Boston has a long history of offering an array of interesting museums to educate and entertain the public. One of the earliest was the five-story Boston Museum of Art, which Philip Woods opened

The Boston Museum of Fine Art, 1890s.

in 1804 on Ann Street. The museum, which had hours Monday to Friday from 9:00 AM to 9:00 PM, featured "Wax Figures, Curiosities, Paintings &c." Some of the prize attractions included "the astonishing invisible Lady, Acoustic Temple, Incomprehensible Crystal, and Reflecting Mirror." Woods also displayed a large crocodile, 12 feet long, which was killed in Egypt, and the "skin of a sea-elephant in natural preservation, which measured eighty feet in length." The museum also featured a theater. According to one early 20th-century writer, Walter Faxon, after visiting the museum, kids would spend a restless night of "strange dreams of wax images, boa constrictors, and 'Aladdin' or 'The Forty Thieves' fused into one composite horror."

A competing museum was Daniel Bowen's museum (Boston's first), which started in 1791 as a wax museum displaying a few figures in the

American Coffee House on State Street and by 1795 was known as the Columbian Museum and had a variety of natural and manmade curiosities in a building at the corner of Bromfield Street and Tremont Street. In 1797, the latest attractions were a wax statue of George Washington in a black suit, and a collection of animated clocks. One featured a canary singing different songs. Another had a chimney sweep and his assistant on top of a chimney, and a third had a butcher killing an ox. This museum burned down in 1803 in a fire whose light could be seen in Portsmouth, New Hampshire, 70 miles away. Bowen started a new museum at Milk and Oliver Streets in 1806, which burned down in 1807. A crowd of spectators gathered in the adjoining cemetery to watch the blaze, but the walls collapsed, killing 10 teenage boys. The museum opened again a few months later and remained open until 1825, when the collection was sold to the New England Museum for $5,000.

The Boston Natural History Museum, 1904.

Create Your Own Museum Display

Boston's museums (and most museums around the country, for that matter) started as collections of cool and interesting stuff. Specimens and artifacts of all kinds were donated or purchased to create large collections. Most of the collections in a museum are stored behind closed doors. Only a fraction, the best and most interesting, is put out on display.

One of the most important functions of a museum is not just to show you things, but also to explain them. The best museums include interesting descriptions of their items on display. In this activity, you'll create your own museum display at home.

YOU'LL NEED

★ Items to display (rocks, coins, comic books, baseball cards, etc.)

★ Index cards

★ Markers

What do you collect? What are you interested in? Rocks? Coins? Stamps? Comics? Baseball cards? Select 10 of the best and most interesting (rare, valuable, cool, etc.) items in your collection to put on display. Find a cabinet, dresser top, or table in your room or home that you can use for the display.

Fold the index cards the long way in the middle so they will stand up. Next, write labels or captions on each card to go with each of your items. The labels should tell the public why your items are so special, giving some history and background. For example, if you put a 1934 dime on display, your caption could be "The Mercury dime was minted in 90 percent silver (and 10 percent copper) between 1916 and 1945. After the death of President Franklin Roosevelt, the dime design was changed to show the deceased president's head. This dime is from 1934, when only 24 million were made. Today more than 2 billion dimes are made every year." You've put the dime into context and made it more interesting.

If your entire exhibit was dimes, you'd want to spread your dime facts around. If not, you could lay on the dime statistics pretty thick for this one item in the display. Your display could be chronological (in date order), thematic (by topic), by color (for rocks and minerals, for example), or arranged the way you think works best. Use display platforms of different heights to create an interesting look, and make sure you have good lighting so visitors can clearly see the display pieces.

Think of any museum you have ever been to and how they use eye-catching displays.

After you have curated, or created, your display, have your family and friends look at your exhibit. See if they have any questions for you.

BOSTON'S GOVERNMENT

The government of the city in 1817 consisted of 9 selectmen who met every Wednesday in Faneuil Hall, a town clerk, a town treasurer, 12 overseers of the poor, a School Committee of 12 people, a superintendent of police, 3 assessors of taxes, a Committee of Finance, 24 fire wards, 15 constables, 2 assay masters, a clerk and inspector of the market, a superintendent of burying grounds, and 14 Board of Health members.

Today, Boston's city government has 69 departments ranging from the Archaeology Department to the Elderly Commission to the Parking Clerk's Office to the Water and Sewer Commission. The city is governed by a mayor and a 13-person city council. Within the mayor's office are 15 cabinets dealing with various aspects of government.

The New England Museum had begun in 1818 on Court Street as a merger of the collections of several other museums in the area, including the Boston Museum and the Boston Linnaean Society, which had been founded in 1815 and featured scientific specimens of natural history from many countries. The Revolutionary War hero General Marquis de Lafayette visited the museum in 1825. In 1832, the price of admission to the New England Museum was 25¢—not a bad price for the time, considering eggs were 15¢ a dozen and milk was 5¢ per quart. The collection was sold in 1839, and in 1841, Moses Kimball founded a new museum called the Boston Museum on Tremont Street. The Boston Museum included a collection of stuffed birds and animals, some Greek sculptures, and paintings.

Donations to the museum in 1852 included fossils of fish, a 16-volume set of books on the "Voyage of the Astrolabe and Zelee," a male peacock, the bones of a "gigantic bird" from New Zealand, 1,500 shells from the eastern seas, a cast of fossil dinosaur tracks, and jars and bottles of reptile specimens. By 1853, the collection had 2,000 specimens of minerals, 6,000 species of plants, 5,000 species of bugs and insects, 1,400 mounted birds, 20,000 shells, and 200 species of reptiles.

Over the years, other popular museums opened in Boston. One of the most notable is the Boston Museum of Fine Art, which opened in 1876 in Copley Square. It has expanded from an original collection of 5,000 works of art to a new home on Huntington Avenue (it relocated in 1909) and more than 500,000 works of art. In 1908, it had 250,000 visitors per year; today more than a million people visit the museum every year.

Science museums have deep roots in the city, beginning in 1780 with the formation of the Academy of Arts and Sciences. In 1801, a society was founded to study natural philosophy and natural history. Its members included future president John Quincy Adams, but the society lasted only until 1807. In 1830, the opening of the Boston Society of Natural History (later known as the New England Museum of Natural History) marked the beginning of what is today's Museum of Science, which attracts 1½ million visitors annually.

Charles River Bridge v. Warren Bridge

One of the most important US Supreme Court cases of the 19th century revolved around two Boston bridges, but the origins of the case went all the way back to the year 1650, when Harvard College was granted the right to operate a ferry from Charlestown to Boston and use the revenue to help pay for the cost of operating the school. The ferry operated successfully for many years, but by the late 18th century, many people felt a bridge would be a more efficient means of crossing the river. In 1785, the Massachusetts legislature incorporated a company specifically to build a bridge over the Charles River. The law granted the company the right to collect tolls on the bridge until 1855, and each year it was to pay some of the proceeds to Harvard University (it was officially recognized as a university in 1780). After 70 years, the bridge would become the property of Massachusetts.

Everything went smoothly until 1828, when the Massachusetts legislature decided to authorize another bridge across the river. The newly created Warren River Bridge Company would be allowed to collect tolls for six years, after which passage over the bridge (which was only 800 feet away from the other bridge) would become free. When the owners of the Charles River Bridge Company heard about the plans for the new bridge, they were furious. They realized that all their paying customers would soon be using the new, free bridge. They would lose almost 20 years of tolls that they had been counting on!

The owners of the Charles River Bridge Company were desperate. They filed suit in the Massachusetts Supreme Court to prevent a new bridge from being built, and when that did not work, they filed for monetary damages. They believed that their contract had been violated. The Massachusetts Supreme Court dismissed their claim, and the lawsuit wound up in the US Supreme Court in 1837.

The great orator Daniel Webster argued for the Charles River Bridge Company. Chief Justice Roger Taney wrote the decision for the majority. He pointed out that though Harvard may have had exclusive rights to operate a ferry, there was no longer any ferry. Those rights had vanished when the bridge was constructed. "The exclusive privileges, if they had such, must follow the fate of the ferry, and can have no legal existence without it," he wrote. Taney explained that the ferry and the bridge were each established by separate grants. There was no connection between the privileges of one and the privileges of the other. The bridge charter had to be interpreted on its own merit, without any consideration of the 1650 charter.

The state could not be restricted in its ability to promote the health and happiness of its citizens. It could not be bound for 70 years from creating any improvements. The country was "free, active, and enterprising, continually advancing in numbers and wealth," and in such a situation "new channels of communication are daily found necessary, both for travel and trade, and are essential to the comfort, convenience, and prosperity of the people."

The government would be wrong to assign control of a river crossing to a single company for a period of 70 years. "While the rights of private property are sacredly guarded, we must not forget that the community also have rights, and that the happiness and wellbeing of every citizen depends on their faithful preservation."

The 1785 charter granted rights to build and operate one bridge for a 70-year period. If anything else happened around the bridge, or the city changed, that didn't matter. Turnpike roads had been built and rebuilt, and railroads replaced turnpike roads. In those circumstances, no company should have thought it had exclusive rights or was entitled to damages because improvements were made. Taney worried that if the Court decided in favor of the Charles River Bridge Company, the country's technology would go back to the technology of the 18th century. All the old and defunct turnpike companies would rise from the dead and bring their claims to court. America would be "obliged to stand still until the claims of the old turnpike corporations shall be satisfied and they shall consent to permit these States to avail themselves of the lights of modern science."

The Broad Street Riot of 1837

It was June 11, 1837, and a fire had raged in the Roxbury section of Boston. The firemen who had been on the scene were just returning to the firehouse on East Street with their engine when an Irish funeral procession went past. One of the firemen who stood in the road was pushed out of the way by an Irishman, and a brawl started. What started as a war of words escalated into physical violence. Firemen rushed to help their friend, and the people in the funeral procession rallied around the man who had shoved the fireman. The Irish funeral-goers eventually took the fire engine from the firehouse and overturned it.

The firemen went to various churches and rang the bells to sound the call for more firemen to join the scene. As more and more men joined the conflict, the Irish hurried to Robbins' wood-wharf and retrieved sticks of wood and large pieces of coal. The Irish wound up on Fort Hill and rained down the sticks and stones on the firemen for a half hour before the firemen rushed the hill and drove the Irishmen onto Broad Street, where the fighting continued for hours. The firemen followed the Irishmen into their homes, breaking windows and smashing furniture. They threw ripped-up beds out of the houses, and the air was thick with straw and feathers. The riot finally died down after the mayor called on the military and 800 cavalry soldiers armed with bayonets arrived on the scene.

An official investigation laid the blame equally on both the firemen and the Irishmen. More than 15,000 people took part in this massive riot, but miraculously, nobody was killed.

From Anti-Antislavery to Pro-Antislavery

In 1783, the Massachusetts Supreme Court ruled that the state's 1780 constitution, with its wording "all men are born free and equal," meant that slavery was not valid. Boston was a hotbed of antislavery activity. In 1831, a dozen Boston abolitionists met and formed the Massachusetts Anti-Slavery Society. But not everyone fully embraced the work of this society and of William Lloyd Garrison, a prominent Massachusetts-born abolitionist.

Anti-abolitionist feelings in Boston came to a head in 1835. In August, about 1,500 Bostonians gathered to denounce the work of the abolitionists as endangering the preservation of the Union. Some Boston merchants were also wary of losing their Southern trade partners. One Boston lawyer printed a pamphlet expressing hope that Massachusetts would enact a law that made it illegal to print antislavery materials or hold antislavery meetings.

In October, a large mob disrupted a meeting of the Boston Female Antislavery Society and prevented about 100 women from entering the meeting site on Washington Street after the first 25 women managed to get in. The mob was looking for George Thompson, a prominent English abolitionist they thought would be there based on an announcement in the *Commercial Gazette* (and flyers posted around Boston) that stated, "The infamous foreign scoundrel will hold forth this afternoon . . . a purse of $100 has been raised by a number of patriotic citizens to reward the individual who shall first lay violent hands on Thompson." Even though it was a mistake and Thompson was not in Boston that day, the mob persisted.

The mayor arrived at the scene and with the police tried to get the mob to dissipate. The mayor urged the women to adjourn their meeting. "Do you wish to see a scene of bloodshed, and confusion?" he asked them. One of the women accused the mayor of having friends who instigated the mob and asked him to sway them to leave, but the mayor denied it. Finally, the women agreed to leave and allowed the police to lead them to safety. But the mob now wanted Garrison, who was in the building and had been scheduled to speak to the women.

Garrison jumped out a back window and onto the roof of a neighboring shed, and from there he went into a carpenter's shop to hide. As he ran up the stairs to the second floor, several rioters found him and tied him with rope. After considering throwing him from the window, they decided to let Garrison go down a ladder. He managed to wriggle free and was escorted by "two or three powerful men, to whose firmness, policy, and muscular energy I am probably indebted for my preservation," as he wrote. The men led Garrison safely to the City Hall, all the while yelling, "He sha'n't be hurt! Don't hurt him! He is an American!" Once Garrison was at City Hall, the mayor decided it would be best for the public safety if he was thrown in jail.

In the years that followed, the situation in the country changed, and many more Northerners were against slavery. Now they saw slavery, not antislavery, as a threat to the Union. This tension came to a head in 1854, when a fugitive slave from Virginia who had been living in Boston was captured and imprisoned under the Fugitive Slave Act. The capture of this 19-year-old African American man, Anthony Burns, incited anger among Bostonians. An ad was placed in the Boston newspapers proclaiming, "A MAN KIDNAPPED—A Public Meeting will be held at Faneuil Hall this evening, May 26, at 7 o'clock, to secure justice for a claimed as a slave by a Virginia kidnapper." A crowd of 500 people packed Faneuil Hall to listen to speeches at the meeting. One of the speakers proposed that the crowd meet in front of the courthouse the next day, but the crowd wanted to go there immediately. When the meeting adjourned, the angry Bostonians made their way to the courthouse, where they were anxious to free Burns from jail. They used a makeshift battering ram and two axes to break into the building. In the chaos that followed, people in the crowd fired shots and one court employee was killed by a bullet. Led by a Virginia-born black Boston Baptist church minister named Leonard Grimes, a group of citizens raised the $1,200 that the slave's owner said

A statue of William Lloyd Garrison in Boston, 1904.

Burns was worth, so they could buy his freedom, but the owner changed his mind and decided not to sell. Burns was accompanied to the waterfront, where a steamer was waiting to take him back to Virginia. The uproar over his deportation was so great that Burns had to be accompanied by a procession of federal troops and marines, as thousands of people watched and jeered.

After he arrived in Virginia, Burns was sold to another slaveholder, but Grimes was able to buy him from that man. Burns moved back to Boston and was given an anonymous scholarship to Oberlin College. He died of tuberculosis at age 28.

Boston's role in the advancement of African American freedoms and rights continued over the years that followed. The First National Conference of the Colored Women of America was held in Boston in 1895. Speakers included Margaret Murray Washington, the wife of Booker T. Washington, one of the prominent African American leaders of the time. The National Federation of Afro-American Women was founded during this conference; it would merge with other groups the next year to form the National Association of Colored Women. Today, African Americans make up about 25 percent of Boston's population.

5

A TIME OF GROWTH

DURING THE CIVIL WAR, many Bostonians worried that their city was unprepared to defend against a Confederate attack. Thankfully, an attack never occurred. However, an accident a decade later caused major damage to the city. The Great Fire of 1872 destroyed 60 acres of Boston. The city quickly rebuilt, and other improvements followed in the decades after, including the great Boston Common park, as well as the Boston subway, which sped up travel.

The Boston Public Garden in 1906.

Civil War Woes

When the Civil War broke out in 1861, New Englanders were worried. The fact that Boston was in the far north didn't mean it was not susceptible to Confederate attack. While a land-based assault was very unlikely, as a port city, Boston was very vulnerable to an attack from the sea.

Governor John Andrew finally decided to take the matter directly to the president. He wrote Abraham Lincoln a long and heartfelt letter, asking the president to "consider the importance of detailing immediately an iron-clad vessel of war for the exclusive duty of protecting the harbors on the Massachusetts coast, and particularly the harbor of Boston." He explained that within firing range of the State House were a population of 500,000 people and important federal buildings such as the Custom House, the Sub-Treasury, the Navy Yard, and the Arsenal at Watertown. He complained that Boston's fortifications had only 20 percent of the proper levels of armament. In Fort Warren and at Castle Island there was not a single gun of more than eight-inch caliber, and the guns that did exist were old and in bad condition. He also mentioned that no federal warships were on the Massachusetts coast for protection.

The governor sent one of his staff members to Washington to take up the matter with the Massachusetts delegation to Congress and with the navy and war departments, but still nothing was done. Though the federal government never sent a ship to guard the city's harbor, the forts mounted more and heavier guns and before the close of the year "were completely armed in the best possible manner," according to a report at the time.

An 1863 letter confiscated from a Confederate soldier by a Union soldier had some alarming information:

President Davis was here a few days ago, and said that the "Alabama," with four others [ships] that will be dreaded as much as she has been, will make the Yankees a call some time in June, at Boston or Portland; and won't they shell out? Davis said the forts might try to play ball a little, but [the Confederate ships] are so fast sailers they could not hurt them much. Won't Governor Andrew look as black as some of his Southern friends, when one of our big shells just bids him

The Sixth Regiment returns to Boston after a three-month tour of duty in 1861. *Author's collection*

good-morning in the State House. Then Boston people can see how good it is to have their homes destroyed; for, before they can get out any thing at the Navy Yard, we can knock them. Any way, how I should like to see the fun! Now, William, after you have read this, burn it up; don't tell any one what is in it, as the visit must be kept a secret, as it would be rather tough to have them know of it.

Waiting for federal help seemed hopeless. The state would have to spend its own money. In March 1863, the Massachusetts legislature authorized $1 million for the defense of the Massachusetts coastline. This money was used to connect the forts of Boston Harbor via a high-technology telegraph system and to install a system of harbor obstructions that would slow any enemy ships. The city still needed a powerful cannon to defend itself, however. Materials were in short supply in the Union, so the governor decided to contract with a British manufacturer that had been supplying the Confederates with guns. The guns were not the best quality, but they were better than nothing. The government ordered ten 11-inch and twelve 9-inch Blakelys for $32,000. The state ordered another 50 guns from a different British company. These guns were powerful: in one test, a 533-pound cannonball, driven by 50 pounds of gunpowder, penetrated 31 feet into an earthen wall. So heavy were these cannons that when one of them was being hoisted from a barge in England on its way to America, it toppled the crane, fell through the bottom of the barge, and sunk it. There were

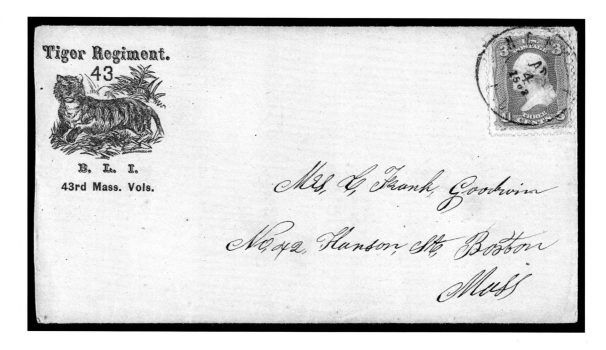

A Civil War envelope from the 43rd Massachusetts Volunteers, mailed to a Boston address.

delays in the delivery of the guns, but thankfully none ever had to be fired, as no attack came.

It was ironic that the state bought guns made by the British. One reason Massachusetts needed guns was because in May 1863, sources told the governor that the British had said if war broke out between Britain and the United States, Portland and Boston would be the first two cities attacked.

The Great Fire of 1872

It was an otherwise calm and ordinary autumn evening in Boston, when at about 7:00 PM on November 9, 1872, a fire suddenly broke out in a four-story granite building on Summer Street. The building housed a wholesale dry goods dealer, a wholesale clothing accessory vendor, and a hoop

Write a Civil War Letter

Massachusetts soldiers played a big part in the Civil War. A total of 159,000 Massachusetts men served in the Union Army between 1861 and 1865. Massachusetts troops served with honor and distinction on battlefields across the country. These New England men found themselves far from home and often lonely. In this activity, you'll imagine you are a Union soldier who has been camping near Washington, DC, for the last few weeks and write a letter to someone at home. The following excerpt is from a letter a New England soldier from the battlefront sent back home in 1864. Many Union men wound up in the Washington, DC, area, at least at first.

While sitting on the east bank of the Potomac last night and hearing the sound of the drum and the roar of the cannon, I thought of home. . . . We are quartered in a beautiful place and can see miles along the Potomac. We can see Georgetown & Georgetown Heights, also Arlington & Arlington Heights & Fort Jackson & Alexandria all on the west bank of the Potomac, & we can see thousands of tents scattered all along on the heights as far as the eye can read & at sunset it is among the beautifulest in my life, & then the Capital & the city is in view in the distance & Fort Washington in the opposite direction which makes a very fine view. We are getting along well now although we had a hard time coming on here and a few days after we camp here but since we came into quarters we get along better, we have plenty to eat now and that is something we didn't get when we first came here, we drill between three and four hours and work as many more so I don't have much time to write and I hasten take my paper on my knapsack or my knee.

Everett M. Arey,
December 1864, Washington DC

YOU'LL NEED

* ★ Looseleaf paper
* ★ Pen
* ★ Backpack filled with clothes

To properly accomplish this activity, try to mimic the conditions under which Arey probably wrote his letter. Go outside at dusk (most likely the time he wrote his letter) with your full backpack, pen, and paper and sit cross-legged on the ground. Lean on your backpack (or your knee) in the fading light and write a letter to your family back home. To make your letter more realistic, first research battles that took place near Washington, and imagine you are taking part in one of them or are on your way to fight.

Remember to update your family on how you are, and also ask how they are and to write back to you. Because of the slow mail delivery during the war, write as if your letter (and their reply) might take a while to arrive at its destination. Not only that, paper was scarce during the war, so use your one sheet well and make each word count. When you are done, fold the paper in eighths so it fits the size envelope you would likely have used back then.

The Great Fire of 1872.

skirt manufacturer. The building had an elevator powered by a small steam engine. A spark from the fire that powered that engine landed and set the basement ablaze, and from there the entire building was aflame.

A fire alarm sounded and fire engines soon arrived at the scene, but the fire was already raging out of control. The building's roof collapsed and sent flames skyward. In less than 20 minutes, the entire facade extending 100 feet along Kingston Street was a sheet of flames. The flames quickly spread in three directions, whipped along by a

fierce wind and encouraged by the wooden roofs of the buildings as well as the densely packed supply of flammable goods in this warehouse district.

The destruction to the city's businesses was incredible. Book publishers, jewelry stores, upholsterers, sewing machine vendors, cutlery showrooms, hat stores, cigar shops, toy warehouses, barber shops, restaurants, banks, and St. Stephen's Church and the old Trinity Church were all destroyed. Some types of business were especially hard hit because they were clustered in the same area. A total of 199 wholesale shoe and

Aftermath of the Great Fire.

boot manufacturers and 159 leather dealers were destroyed. The entire wool trade in Boston was ruined, as a staggering total of 8 million pounds of wool were burned. The fire destroyed more than 75 percent of all the paper warehouses in Boston.

By the time the fire was finally contained the next day, it had burned for 15 hours, killed about 20 people, and destroyed 60 acres of the city. It burned more than $90 million worth of property, including more than 750 buildings and a ship. At least 20,000 young girls who worked in industries that were affected were put out of work.

A *New York Sun* reporter who surveyed the damage said, "I saw iron pillars and beams melted into misshapen masses, granite blocks burnt to ashes, and tin roofs melted. Staircases had run like molten lead." The scene amid the ruins was clogged with a variety of onlookers including insurance appraisers, exhausted policemen and firemen, armed militia, relic hunters and thieves, newly unemployed girls, and merchants without warehouses. Kids who snuck into the rubble hawked (sold) relics of the fire, such as pieces of twisted iron and strips of charred leather.

In the days that followed, more than 1,000 people helped clear the rubble and debris, even as small pockets of fire still smoldered. The City of Chicago, grateful for the assistance that Boston had lent after its own great fire just a year before, offered much kindness and assistance, including $100,000. Boston's resiliency was incredible. Within 12 hours of the fire, hundreds of merchants

Be a Headline Writer

Newspaper headlines are an extremely important component of good news stories. Large, bold, and sometimes in italics or all capital letters, headlines are the first thing a reader sees when picking up a newspaper or reading an online news story. Headlines have to be eye-catching, interesting, and enticing enough to sell newspapers. The more dramatic the news story, the greater potential for powerful and gripping headlines. In this activity, you'll learn to write headlines for one of the events in Boston's history.

YOU'LL NEED

★ 8½-by-11-inch printer paper

★ Pen

★ Computer with word-processing software

★ Printer

One headline often is not enough to capture the full gravity of a story, so in some cases subheads are used. Nineteenth-century newspapers used several headlines for a major story, as was the case in this Connecticut newspaper story about the Great Fire in Boston:

———

AWFUL CALAMITY

BOSTON ON FIRE

MILES ON MILES OF FIRE

A SUBLIME AND AWFUL SIGHT

LOSSES $90,000,000

14 SOLID STREETS GONE

POWDER BLASTS ADD TO THE HORROR

———

And in this one from the *New York Times*:

———

ANOTHER CHICAGO

TERRIBLE AND DESTRUCTIVE FIRE IN

THE CITY OF BOSTON

GRANITE WAREHOUSE MELTED BY INTENSE HEAT

VAIN EFFORTS OF THE FIREMEN TO CHECK THE FLAMES

A NORTH-WEST WIND CARRIES THE FIRE BEFORE IT

THE LOSS ALREADY ESTIMATED AT MILLIONS

STARTLING SCENES OF PANIC AMONG THE PEOPLE

———

Now it's your turn. Pick a historic event from this book and do more research on it if necessary. Imagine you've just written a story about this event. See if you can come up with five to seven headlines to use for your story. Remember, order is important; the top headline is the summary and the ones that follow add important, strange, and interesting details. The headlines should tell the reader the most dramatic highlights of the story that would make them want to read on, without giving everything away.

set off for New York to buy more goods and were already seeking new space to rent in Boston. The burnt section of Boston was rebuilt quickly and the rubble from the fire used as landfill.

Port City

Boston continued to be an important port city throughout the 19th century. In 1852, the ship *Northern Light* set a record for the quickest passage between Boston and San Francisco (around Cape Horn)—52 days. As sailing ships gave way to steamships, Boston remained competitive. In 1877,

100 steamships sailed from Boston to Europe. In 1882, 208 steamships left Boston, and by 1894, the number was up to 360 steamships. Boston was second only to New York as a port of export, and third in the country in imports. In trade with Great Britain, Boston was actually the top port in the country, with 175,000 tons of goods being shipped to England in the year 1894 alone.

The steamships of the late 19th century were huge—about 520 feet long, 55 feet wide, and able to carry 5,000 to 8,000 tons of goods each. To accommodate these larger ships, the main shipping channel in Boston Harbor was widened from

Boston in 1873.

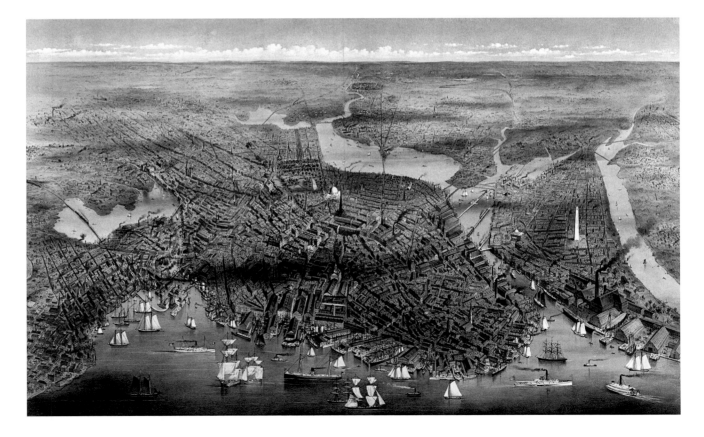

Create a Bill of Lading

Boston has been one of the country's main ports for centuries. Since the 1600s, ships have sailed to and from Boston laden with goods destined for a wide variety of locations. To ensure that the contents of an arriving shipment matched the items ordered and loaded onto the ship, merchants needed a document to check against the cargo and verify the contents were as described. The bill of lading served that purpose. This preprinted document had many blanks for the shipper to fill in with information such as the port of departure and arrival, the contents of the shipment, and other details. The image on this page shows a bill of lading for a ship that originated in Boston, carrying 57 casks of rum to New York. Similar bills of lading are still used today. In this activity, you will design your own bill of lading.

YOU'LL NEED

★ Computer with internet access and word-processing software

★ Printer

★ 8½-by-11-inch printer paper

★ Pen

1. Type the preprinted words from the sample bill of lading into a computer document and leave blanks. Find an image of a ship and insert it in the upper left-hand corner.

2. Print the blank bill of lading on a piece of paper.

3. Have a friend select what type of item he or she would like to receive from you. Research the bulk price of that item and then use the pen to fill in the blanks with the information. For example, if your friend wants chewing gum, see how much it would cost to buy 100 boxes of gum, and enter that price on the form.

4. Fill in your friend's name and yours in the appropriate places and sign the form.

For more fun, with your teacher's help, arrange to create a bill of lading for a shipment of food or supplies that has been ordered for your school. Your class can create a bill of lading to match the order and then examine the contents when the shipment arrives to verify that everything is as described.

An 1860 bill of lading for a ship that sailed from Boston to New York.
Author's collection

558

BLUE STORE

CLOTHING HOUSE.

Jobbers and Retailers of

**GENTLEMEN'S, YOUTHS', BOYS'
AND CHILDREN'S**

Fine New York

CLOTHING.

150, 152, 154, 156, 158, 160, 162, 164

WASHINGTON STREET,

Facing Cornhill and Adams Statue, Boston.

JOSEPH COMER, Proprietor.

600 feet to 1,000 feet and deepened from 23 feet to 27 feet. One of Boston's advantages at the time was that it was 200 miles closer to Europe than any other US port, which shaved at least a day off the travel time.

Besides serving as a port, Boston was known for its shipbuilding. The ship *North American*, finished in East Boston in 1873, was known for its great speed. It made its first voyage from New York to Melbourne, Australia, in just 72 days, which was very impressive. The *South American*, launched in 1876, was another speedy ship built in Boston. It sailed from San Francisco to Liverpool, Hong Kong, and back to San Francisco in 10 months and 17 days, a new record for around-the-world sailing at the time.

Boston in 1884

By 1884, Boston's population was 362,535. The city was large and modern but still old-fashioned in many ways. It was poised for all the changes of the 20th century but still very much a 19th-century metropolis. Boston had 14 electric lighting companies and 20 electricians but 225 coal and wood (for burning) dealers. If you needed a bicycle, you could go to one of seven dealers in the city, but you could still get a hoop skirt at one of three dealers in town. There were 29 companies that manufactured elevators or parts for elevators, but there were also 128 blacksmiths. Horses were still very much a part of the Boston landscape—the city had 68 carriage builders, 43 hay and straw dealers, and 102 harness makers, but was also home to offices of 119 different railroad companies. The communication business thrived as technology improved—6 telegraph companies, 8 telephone companies, and 80 photographers called Boston home, but so did 8 ink dealers.

Boston had an incredible array of shopping options at this time, with over 200 variety stores around the city, let alone the hundreds of other specialty shops such as booksellers, shoe dealers, furriers, hatters, cigar dealers, and piano dealers. All that shopping might build up an appetite, which you could easily satisfy at one of the city's more than 400 restaurants. If you didn't feel like eating out and wanted to cook your own food, you could buy fruit and vegetables from 240 produce dealers and a variety of other food from 520 provision dealers. These days, if you rip a piece of clothing, you are likely to discard it and buy another, but in 19th-century Boston, if you didn't fix it yourself (perhaps using a sewing machine purchased from one of the 38 dealers in town), you would take it to one of the city's 350 tailors.

Italian Immigrants

Though the largest and earliest wave of immigrants to Boston was the Irish, by the end of the 19th century another group was coming to Boston by the thousands: Italians. Of course, some Italians arrived in Boston before then—the Venice-born composer Filippo Traetta (Americanized to Philip Trajetta) arrived in Boston in 1800 and founded the first music academy in the country—but not very many.

Italians, largely from Southern Italy and Sicily, started arriving in larger numbers around 1870 after the unification of Italy failed to provide them with any economic benefits. The Italians were escaping poor economic conditions and heavy taxes. In 1882, the average Italian worker in Italy made $140 per year and was taxed $15.44. Many of the Italian immigrants who went to Boston had their ocean passage paid for by friends or family already in the country; they arrived with an average of nine dollars in their pockets.

They began to settle in the North End, which at the time was home mainly to Irish immigrants. Though at first Italians shared the neighborhood with the Irish and others, by 1930 it was almost exclusively Italian. Very few Italians lived in Boston before 1870, but within three years the Italian population had increased so much that in 1873 the new immigrants built St. Leonard's Church at the corner of Hanover and Prince Streets. It was the first Catholic Church in New England to be founded by Italians.

Nineteenth-century living conditions were very cramped. Nearly all Italian immigrants lived in tightly packed apartment houses called tenements, and over 150 of these Italian immigrant families were each living in just one room. Single men often shared rooms, sometimes with 10 men to a single room, each one paying 25¢ a week. Many Italian immigrant men came to Boston first and sent for their families later. In 1901, for example, almost 80 percent of all Italian immigrants were male. Luckily, these new arrivals had assistance. Immigrants who arrived earlier formed

An Italian-American boy looking for work on Salem Street, 1909.

the country, children of the hardworking immigrants attended school, got good-paying jobs, and became a vital part of Boston.

These days, Little Italy is a vibrant place alive with Italian culture, including numerous restaurants. About 3,000 Italian Americans live in the North End.

The First Irish Mayor

Though the Irish population of Boston was steadily increasing through the mid-19th century, it took years for the Irish to be represented in the Boston city government. In 1870, Christopher Augustus Connor became the first Irish-born city alderman.

Finally, in 1884, Boston elected its first Irish-born mayor. Hugh O'Brien, Boston's 31st mayor, was born in 1827 in Ireland and came to America with his family in 1832. He became involved in the printing and publishing business at the age of 12 when he started working for the *Boston Courier* newspaper, and by the age of 15 he was the foreman of a printing company. He eventually helped found and became part owner of a publication called *The Commercial and Shipping List*. With a growing reputation among Boston's merchants, O'Brien entered politics in 1875 and was elected to a seat on the Board of Aldermen, where he served until 1883. He ran for mayor in 1883 and lost, but won when he ran again the next year.

O'Brien's first term was a success, and when he won reelection in 1885, he beat the Republican candidate by 8,597 votes (59 percent to 41 percent), the largest margin of victory by a mayoral

the Boston Italian Immigrant Society, and society members met the new Italian immigrants at the steamships to offer them aid and supervision.

Many of the arriving Italians were illiterate. Just like the Irish before them, they experienced prejudice, even from unlikely sources. The *Boston Medical and Surgical Journal* in 1887 described the "large numbers of Italian immigrants of the lower classes and filthy habits."

As time passed and their numbers grew, Italians became a major presence in the city. By 1900, over 13,000 people living in Boston had been born in Italy, and 20,000 Bostonians had parents who were born in Italy. Just as in cities around candidate in Boston to that time. He served four one-year terms and then was defeated in 1888 by 2,000 votes. One of his main legacies was advocating for more parkland in Boston. In part through his efforts, the 527-acre Franklin Park, designed by the famous landscape architect Frederick Law Olmsted, was created.

Upon O'Brien's death in 1895, one of his former colleagues, Michael Norris, said, "Elected Mayor of Boston on a distinctly party issue, and as a pronounced Democrat, his administration was purely non-partisan in action. . . . He was a broad-minded, progressive public man, and as Mayor accomplished reforms in the financial departments of our government that benefited every member of the community, and received the commendation of every citizen interested in the welfare of our city." More than 150 priests took part in his funeral service at Holy Cross Cathedral. After O'Brien broke the ice, many other Irish mayors followed, including John Fitzgerald (in office 1895–1901), who was John F. Kennedy's maternal grandfather; Patrick Collins (1902–1905); Daniel Whelton (1905–1906); and others. The predominance of Irish mayors in Boston has continued with Mayor Marty Walsh, who was elected in 2013 and 2017.

Boston Subway

By the late 19th century, transportation in Boston was becoming a critical issue. With a population of 500,000 in the city itself and another 500,000 in the suburbs, moving people from one place to another was becoming a priority for the city. In 1889, what was meant to be an improvement when the streetcars were switched from horsepower to electric power actually made things worse. What was supposed to be faster and more comfortable service drew more people to use the system, which increased congestion. Boston's main streets were blocked by lines of streetcars, and service was painfully slow. The streetcar system was overloaded, making Boston's streets a crowded mess.

In 1891, a rapid transit commission was appointed to examine the problem. The commission studied the situation and proposed a few different ideas. One was a new central avenue between Washington and Tremont Streets where all streetcar traffic could run, but this would have

Hugh O'Brien.
Author's collection

Make a Boston Cream Pie

Over the years, several popular dishes have originated in Boston. Boston baked beans are one delicious Massachusetts specialty, and Boston cream pie is another. The "pie" is actually a sponge cake that is filled with cream and covered in chocolate. According to popular legend, it was invented by a chef at the Parker House Hotel in 1855, but its origins actually go back to at least 1846 and a recipe for Boston cream cake. It was also known as Martha Washington pie. Though more recent recipes include chocolate frosting, 19th-century cookbook recipes do not mention chocolate. In 1996, Boston cream pie was named the official state dessert of Massachusetts. It was also the favorite dessert of the Kennedy family.

Try your hand at making this sweet treat! The recipe below is adapted from the White House Cook Book, *which first came out in the 1880s and was written by a former White House chef, but you can certainly locate other, more modern versions of the recipe if you wish.*

ADULT SUPERVISION REQUIRED

INGREDIENTS

For the cream:

★ 1 cup sugar
★ ½ cup flour
★ 2 eggs
★ 1 pint milk
★ 2 tablespoons butter
★ 1 teaspoon vanilla extract or lemon juice

For the cake:

★ 1 cup sugar
★ 1½ cups flour, sifted
★ 1 heaping teaspoon baking powder
★ 3 eggs
★ 2 tablespoons milk or water
★ 1 teaspoon vanilla extract or lemon juice
★ Butter, vegetable oil, or cooking spray

MATERIALS

★ 2–4 mixing bowls
★ Fork or whisk
★ Rubber spatula
★ Small saucepan
★ Stove
★ Measuring spoons
★ Electric mixer
★ 2 standard metal or glass pie plates (8 or 9 inches)
★ Oven
★ Sharp, broad-bladed knife

For the cream:

1. In a mixing bowl, using a fork or whisk, combine 1 cup of sugar with ½ cup of flour.
2. In a separate mixing bowl, lightly beat two eggs with a fork or whisk. Then add the sugar and flour mixture to the eggs and mix well with a rubber spatula.
3. In a small saucepan, bring 1 pint of milk to a boil on the stove over medium heat.
4. Using a whisk, stir the egg mixture into the milk.
5. Add 2 tablespoons of butter and stir in one continuous direction until the mixture thickens.
6. Stir in 1 teaspoon of vanilla extract or lemon juice.
7. Remove from the heat and set aside to cool.

For the cake:

1. Mix together 1 cup of sugar, 1½ cups of sifted flour, and 1 heaping teaspoon of baking powder.
2. Separate the whites from the yolks of three eggs, putting the whites in one bowl and the yolks in another.
3. Beat the yolks with 2 tablespoons of milk or water and 1 teaspoon of vanilla or lemon (whichever you used to flavor the cream).
4. Add the sugar and flour mixture to the yolks and mix until smooth.
5. Beat the egg whites with an electric mixer until they are stiff and form peaks.
6. Fold the whites into the yolk mixture with a spatula, a little at a time, and gently mix together until all is incorporated.
7. Grease the two pie plates with butter, vegetable oil, or cooking spray and pour half the batter into each pie plate.
8. Bake at 375 degrees until golden (about 20 minutes). Test for doneness by piercing the center of the cake with a toothpick. If the toothpick comes out clean, the cake is done. If not, test it again five minutes later. Allow to cool completely.
9. With a sharp, broad-bladed knife, carefully slice each cake along the center, making two layers of each.
10. Using a spatula, spread half the cream between the layers of one cake. Repeat with the second cake.
11. Serve cold.

cost a lot of money, damaged many buildings, and still caused problems where the tracks crossed existing roads. The commission found that the best option was a subway—it would destroy almost no property, eliminate the danger of crossing tracks on street level, make navigating the streets less crowded and confusing by removing all rails, decrease noise, and be cheaper than widening the streets to allow for new surface tracks.

On March 28, 1895, the first spadeful of earth was removed to build the subway. Boston's subway system would be the first in America, and only the third in the world after London's and Budapest's. The construction method was cut-and-cover, which involves an open excavation to build the tunnel sections. Once the street was excavated, a series of vertical and then horizontal support beams were placed, and then a concrete arch roof was placed over the tunnel shell, followed by a layer of fill and then asphalt. It was not an especially deep subway. The rails were only 17 feet below the surface of the street.

One obstacle workers faced during construction was the cemeteries along the subway route. The bones of 910 people had to be removed and reburied before construction of the first segment of subway. Other than that, the work went fairly smoothly, with one terrible exception. A tragic accident occurred on March 4, 1897, when a gas leak from street-level pipes caused gas to build up in a pocket between the subway roof and the temporary street surface and then ignite from the spark of an electric streetcar's wheel. The result was a tremendous explosion at the corner of Tremont and Boylston Streets. The streetcar became airborne, then fell to the ground. Flames shot up and debris flew 200 feet into the air. So many windows were shattered in the vicinity that 39 tons of glass were needed to replace them all. Curiosity drew many people to the site, and 150 policemen were required to keep the crowds back after the explosion. Nine people were killed and dozens injured. It was deemed the gas company's fault and unrelated to the subway construction itself.

The subway opened on September 1, 1897, with

FAMOUS BOSTONIANS

Many celebrities were born in Boston. They include, of course, numerous patriotic Revolutionary-era figures, such as Paul Revere, Samuel Adams, John Hancock, and Benjamin Franklin. The list also includes many well-known writers such as E. E. Cummings, Henry David Thoreau, Edgar Allan Poe, and Nathaniel Hawthorne. Boston is also the birthplace of some of the best-known musical acts of all time, including Aerosmith, Boston, James Taylor, and the Cars.

The list of Boston-born actors is long and impressive and includes film stars Matt Damon, Anthony Michael Hall, Uma Thurman, James Spader, and Mark Wahlberg; Leonard "Spock" Nimoy of *Star Trek*; late night TV host Conan O'Brien; and stars of the popular television show *The Office* John Krasinski and Mindy Kaling. The artist Winslow Homer was a Boston native, as was artist and inventor Samuel Morse.

Edgar Allan Poe was born in Boston.

Copyright 1905 by the Rotograph Co.

Park Street subway entrances, 1905.

additional sections completed in 1898. The first segment completed, the Tremont Street Subway, included five stations: at the corner of Boylston and Tremont, the corner of Tremont and Park, Brattle Square, Haymarket Square, and Canal Street (across from the Union Depot).

The subway was an immediate success. In October 1898, an average of 64,000 subway fares were sold per day, nearly 2 million for the month, with 3.6 million free transfers! An estimated 50 million people used the subway in its first year. People could get around Boston much more efficiently, and the streets were less congested.

In the years that followed, the city constructed more transit segments, including elevated lines and subways. Eventually, the elevated routes were abandoned in favor of additional subways. Today, the subway system, run by the Massachusetts Bay Transportation Authority (MBTA), is considered one of the best in the world and consists of 145 stations on five different lines, extending from as far south as Braintree to as far north as Oak Grove.

The Boston Public Garden

When the Boston Common was first created as a public ground in the 17th century, it was on the northwestern edge of the city. The Common's northern border was the Charles River, and to the west was marshland. The Mill Dam was built in 1821 so that some of the land could be reclaimed, but that was not enough.

Two hundred years later a new public garden was built on the western edge of the Common, on what was once nothing but foul-smelling tidal marshes (and later, after the land was filled in, mud flats) near Charles Street by the Charles River. In 1837, the city leased 20 acres of land to a

BOSTON LETTUCE

What is Boston lettuce? The history of this leafy green dates back to the 19th century, when lettuce was the largest cash crop grown by market gardeners in Massachusetts, especially those with greenhouses. Lettuce was grown year-round, both outdoors and indoors. According to an 1895 agriculture report by W. W. Rawson of Arlington, Massachusetts:

By some growers it is a daily article to carry to market. The seed is sown every week by those who make a business of it, and as the weather grows cool in the fall, it is transplanted into houses built for the purpose. The Massachusetts market gardener supplies not only Boston market, but New York, Philadelphia, Washington, and Chicago, with his lettuce. We grow the headed variety, and it cannot be grown as well in other localities, and therefore the term "Boston Lettuce" is applied to it.

group that wanted to create a botanical garden on the site. The group built a greenhouse and planted ornamental trees. A former circus building north of Beacon Street and west of Charles Street was converted into a conservatory for plants and birds, but it burned down. There were many wondrous attractions in the garden, including a bed of prize tulips imported from England and valued at $1,500. Because part of the land was still marshy and uneven, only some of the garden was formally landscaped.

Though the garden was successful, the group operating it turned the land back to the city in 1852 due to financial troubles. In 1859, the citizens of Boston voted to keep the garden land public for all eternity. They hired George F. Meacham, who had won a $100 prize for his design, to create its layout. The landscaped park included a large pond and numerous walking paths. Though some in the city government suggested adding public buildings to the park, the idea was rejected. An iron fence was erected around the park in 1862. In 1863, the city government created the position of parks superintendent to oversee the Public Garden, Common, and other parks. Improvements and additions continued to be made over the years.

A scenic bridge was added to the pond in 1867, and the park's first statue, the Ether Monument, a monument to the discovery of the use of ether for anesthesia, was installed in 1868, followed by an equestrian statue of George Washington in 1869. By 1881, the garden had 90,000 plants and 1,500 trees.

The Swan Boats

The attractive lagoon in the Boston Public Garden is the perfect place for a leisurely row in a small boat. In 1877, Robert Paget was among those who introduced a new kind of boat to the lagoon. The boat was propelled by a paddle wheel that an operator moved using pedals. But how could he make the boat more attractive? He was inspired by an opera called *Lohengrin*, in which the hero crosses a river in a boat drawn by a swan. The boats would feature a giant swan cutout on either side, to partially hide the operator. The idea was a tremendous hit, and although Robert Paget died in 1878, his widow took over the business and it has remained in the family since then.

The first swan boats had one seat, but later the floats were enlarged to include three iron settees holding three people each. The boats were powered by a paddler. During the day, they were shaded by an awning, and after the boating season ended, they were taken apart and stored for the winter.

These rides were popular with children and adults alike. When a local newspaper advertised free tickets in the summer of 1894, a crowd of 4,000 boys and girls waited in line for the chance to go on a swan boat for free. In 1895, there were three swan boats and a fourth under construction. In 1902 and 1903, the well-known wealthy Bostonian Arthur Dixwell donated 200 tickets for the swan boats to the Children's Aid Society of Boston. Business was booming, and by 1915 the Pagets were taking in nearly $5,000 a year in receipts from the swan boat rides.

The swan boats were made even more famous by Robert McCloskley's award-winning 1941 children's book *Make Way for Ducklings*, about a pair of mallards who decide to raise their ducklings in

The swan boats circa 1900.

the Boston Public Garden lagoon and mistake the swan boats for real swans. The current fleet of six swan boats are larger reproductions of the originals, holding 20 passengers each, and date from 1910 to 1956. The ride lasts 15 minutes, and has been taken by celebrities including Shirley Temple, Calvin Coolidge, and John F. Kennedy. The swan boats were designated a Boston landmark in 2011.

The Mother of Measurement

Born in Boston in 1857, Fannie Merritt Farmer suffered a paralytic stroke as a teenager and for a long time could not walk. She eventually regained her health and began cooking for her mother's boardinghouse. She enjoyed cooking so much that she wanted to learn more and eventually attended the Boston Cooking School, graduating at the age of 32. A star pupil, before long she was named as director of the school. In 1896, she published a groundbreaking cookbook with her own money.

There had been plenty of cookbooks before hers, but the nearly 2,000-recipe *Boston Cooking School Cookbook* was the first to standardize measurements. Fannie Farmer introduced the concept of the "level" measurement. By her reckoning, a teaspoon of flour had to be leveled flat with a knife. This way everyone would use the same amount, rather than whatever heaping amount of flour a teaspoon might hold after being dipped into the flour container.

Farmer also explained the science of cooking, teaching readers how to build a good fire on a wood-burning stove, properly fry foods, and best combine ingredients. As she explained in the book's preface, "It is my wish that it may not only be looked upon as a compilation of tried and tested recipes, but that it may awaken an interest through its condensed scientific knowledge which will lead to deeper thought and broader study of what to eat."

The first brownie recipe was published in the 1906 edition of the book. After an initial print run of just 3,000 copies, the book went on to sell 360,000 copies by the time of Farmer's death in 1915.

Level Measurement Experiment

Boston Cooking School Cookbook *author Fannie Farmer helped standardize cooking measurements by using the "flat" measurement as the standard in her recipes. In this experiment, you will see just how much of a difference this can make in cooking. When people use different amounts of ingredients such as salt or baking soda in baking a cake, for example, it can make a big difference in the cake's flavor and density.*

YOU'LL NEED

★ Tablespoon measuring spoon

★ ½ tablespoon measuring spoon

★ Flour

★ 2 small bowls

★ Butter knife

1. Remove a heaping tablespoon of flour, and deposit it into a small bowl. (A heaping spoon is whatever you can successfully "carry" on the spoon.) Repeat until you have 3 heaping tablespoons of flour in the bowl.

2. Now it's time to measure how many flat tablespoons of flour you have in the bowl. Remove a tablespoon of flour from the bowl. This time, level it off with a butter knife so that the top is flat. Allow the excess flour to fall back into the bowl. Put the flat tablespoon of flour into a second bowl.

3. Repeat this until you have moved all the flour to the second bowl, keeping track of how many flat tablespoons you've removed. (When you have less than a tablespoon left in the first bowl, use the ½ tablespoon for the rest.)

4. How many flat tablespoons was your 3 heaping tablespoons equal to? How much more flour did the rounded tablespoon amount to versus the flat tablespoon? To calculate this percentage, subtract 3 (the number of heaping tablespoons) from the number of flat tablespoons, and then divide that total by 3. For example, if the flour in the cup amounted to 5 flat tablespoons, the calculation would look like this:

$$5 - 3 = 2$$
$$2 \div 3 = .6666666$$

Rounding the decimal up, you have 67 percent more flour using rounded tablespoons than flat tablespoons.

MODERN BOSTON

THE 20TH CENTURY was a time of great change and modernization in Boston. The skyline changed dramatically as skyscrapers rose and dwarfed the church spires and ships' masts that had long been the tallest structures in the city. Downtown Boston was split by a new highway that was supposed to improve transportation but in the end became a traffic-filled blight and was replaced by a tunnel. Meanwhile, the city was home to several political dynasties and yielded one president and two presidential candidates.

Boston in 1964.

The Police Strike

In the early 20th century, labor unions were on the rise. Workers around the country were unionizing because they felt banding together would give them a stronger voice to get better working conditions and higher wages. In August 1919, the Boston police force formed a union under the American Federation of Labor. They wanted better pay and more sanitary working conditions at their station houses. They claimed the stations were cramped and dirty and that they brought home bugs in their clothes.

Governor Calvin Coolidge in 1919. His tough stance on the striking policemen helped boost his popularity. He later became president.

When police commissioner Edwin Curtis found out about this new union, he pointed to a rule that forbade the police from joining any outside organization. Curtis promptly announced that 19 of the union leaders would be tried for violating the rule. The police union threatened to strike if any disciplinary action was taken against the officers. Curtis's response was to put out a call for volunteers for an unpaid police reserve, just in case. A Harvard professor of physics was the first to sign up.

At 5:45 PM on September 9, 1919, the commissioner announced that the 19 policemen were suspended. The police union met that night and voted to go on strike by a vote of 1,134 to 2. A total of 1,117 of the 1,544 police on the force instantly walked off, turned in their badges, and left their station houses, leaving the city largely unprotected. Though it was relatively calm at first, the next night violence and looting broke out across the city. Robbers made away with small fortunes. Though thousands of volunteers had signed up for the police reserve, they were inexperienced men without the authority of uniforms. The mayor called out the 1,000 members of the State Guard, and Governor Calvin Coolidge increased it to all of the State Guard. They took to the streets with rifles and bayonets. By Thursday, September 11, 7,000 members of the State Guard were in Boston.

A furious Coolidge viewed the men not as strikers but as deserters. He said, "There is no right to strike against the public safety by anybody, anywhere, any time." President Woodrow

Wilson said it was "a crime against civilization." On September 12, Samuel Gompers, president of the American Federation of Labor, asked Coolidge to reinstate the police, but Coolidge refused. It took until December 12 for the last of the state guardsmen to withdraw from Boston. Coolidge's popularity soared as a result of his hard-line handling of the strike. He was reelected governor by a wide margin two months after the strike and soon after became vice president of the United States.

Skyscrapers

Boston has never been quite the skyscraper city like Chicago or New York, but it certainly has its share of tall buildings. Boston's first skyscraper, the 13-story Ames Building, was built in 1893. A city ordinance in the early 20th century limited the height of buildings to 12 stories, but the US government ignored that limit in 1915 when the 30-story, 502-foot-high Boston Custom House was built, replacing the Ames Building as Boston's tallest. With its 21-foot-diameter clock dial, the tower is visible for miles.

The real skyscraper boom in Boston came in the 1960s and '70s, starting with the 749-foot-high (907 feet with its antenna) Prudential Tower in 1964 and the 601-foot-high One Boston Place in 1970. The Prudential Tower has an observatory at its summit, offering panoramic views of Boston.

The city's tallest (and New England's tallest) building today is the 60-story, 790-foot-high 200 Clarendon Street (originally known as the Hancock Tower), designed by I. M. Pei and completed

The Custom House Tower was once the tallest building in Boston.

The Prudential Center in 1964.

in 1976, eight years after the first shovel of dirt was turned. Though 200 Clarendon Street does not even make the list of the 50 tallest buildings in the United States, it is a beloved star of the Boston skyline. This icon is a photographer's favorite due to its mirrorlike glass windows, which were a serious issue during construction when the original glass panes began to pop out of their frames and eventually had to be replaced—all 10,000 of them.

Boston Baseball

Boston's first professional baseball team dates all the way back to the formation of the National Association of Professional Base Ball Players in 1871. The team was called the Boston Red Stockings because it was made up of a core of players from the country's first professional baseball team, the Cincinnati Red Stockings, which had debuted in 1869 and dissolved the next year. The Red Stockings won four championships before joining the newly formed National League (NL) in 1876. In their debut NL year, the Boston Red Stockings won 39 games and lost 31, good enough for fourth place in a league of eight teams. The next two years the Red Stockings finished in first place, to the joy of Bostonians.

The team changed its name several times in the years that followed. They were known as the Boston Beaneaters from 1883 to 1906 and enjoyed some success, finishing in first place five times between 1891 and 1898. The name changed again to the Boston Doves in 1907, the Boston Rustlers in 1911, and then the Boston Braves in 1912. The

Babe Ruth (far left) as a member of the Red Sox, 1915.

name changed to the Boston Bees in 1936 and back to the Braves again in 1941.

The Braves won the World Series just once, in 1914, and were for the most part a consistently mediocre or bad team, except for a World Series appearance in 1948 (when they lost to the Cleveland Indians). In 1953, dwindling fan interest in the team sent the Braves packing to Milwaukee and eventually, in 1966, to Atlanta, where they remain today.

Boston's American League (AL) team, the Red Sox, dates back to the formation of the AL in 1901. Their stadium, the beloved Fenway Park, was built in 1912, and is baseball's oldest ballpark. The Red Sox have had many great players over the years, but perhaps the greatest of them made his biggest mark after leaving the team. The great slugger

Babe Ruth began his major league career in Boston as a pitcher, and a very fine one at that. He came to the Sox as a 19-year-old in 1914 when the team's owner, Joseph Lannin, purchased Ruth's contract from a minor league team. In six years with Boston, Ruth had an incredible 89–46 record. Though the Sox won several World Series, in 1915, 1916, and 1918, with Babe Ruth leading the charge, he wound up on the New York Yankees in 1920 after the Red Sox sold him for $100,000.

Although Ruth did pitch in (and win) five more games during his career in New York, his conversion to an outfielder and a hitter was his claim to fame. Giving up Ruth led to what many baseball fans claimed to be a curse on the Red Sox. The team appeared in the World Series only three times between 1919 and 2003, losing each time.

Superstar Ted Williams played for the Red Sox his entire career. *Author's collection*

But the Curse of the Bambino was finally broken in 2004, when the Red Sox beat the St. Louis Cardinals four games to none. They won the World Series again in 2007 and 2013.

Besides Babe Ruth, another outstanding Red Sox player was Ted Williams, a lifetime Boston fixture. During his 19-year career, interrupted by distinguished service in World War II and Korea, he batted .344 and hit 521 home runs. He was the last player to hit over .400 in a season, which he accomplished in 1941.

James Curley

There have been many figures in Boston's political history, but none with as wide-ranging and sometimes disappointment-filled career as James Michael Curley. Curley had a 50-year career in Boston politics with many ambitions, not all of them met.

Born in 1874, Curley started his career as a sales representative for a baking and confectionary company but soon got into politics. After a few unsuccessful attempts in the late 1890s, he served as a member of the Boston Common Council from 1900 to 1902, served in the State House of Representatives from 1902 to 1904, was a member of the Boston Board of Aldermen from 1904 to 1910, and was a member of the Boston City Council from 1910 to 1912.

This time was not all happy for Curley. In 1904, he was thrown in jail after he was found guilty of taking a federal civil service exam for one of his constituents who wanted to be a letter carrier.

Calculate Home Run Percentage

Baseball's best-known slugger, the Yankee Babe Ruth, started out with the Boston Red Sox as a pitcher. Ruth was an excellent pitcher, but it soon became clear that he had another talent: hitting. By 1918, he led the league in home runs with 11, and in 1919, he whacked 29 homers, also for the league lead. The thing to remember is that he managed to do this even while he was still pitching and not getting as many at bats as a position player would. So how can we tell just how much of a home run hitter Ruth was, knowing he didn't play full time? A rarely used statistic called home run percentage is the way.

While batting average tells how well a player hits in general and slugging average tells how prone someone is to hitting extra base hits, home run percentage is a very clear and simple measure of how often someone hits homers. It is simply the number of home runs divided by the number of at bats, multiplied by 100 and then rounded to one decimal place. In 1918, Ruth had 11 homers in 317 at bats.

$$11 \div 317 = 0.0347$$
$$0.0347 \times 100 = 3.5$$

In 1918 Ruth had a 3.5 home run percentage—meaning he hit home runs 3.5 percent of the time, or 3.5 times in every 100 at bats.

In 1919, his percentage went up to 6.7 percent. But Ruth was just getting started. His numbers kept increasing, and by 1927 with the Yankees, his home run percentage was a whopping 11.1 percent.

The career leader in home run percentage is Mark McGwire at 9.4 percent, followed by Babe Ruth at 8.5 percent.

Now that you know how to calculate home run percentage, see if you can figure out the percentage for Red Sox slugging star Ted Williams in the following years:

    1941: 37 homers in 456 AB
    1942: 36 homers in 522 AB
    1949: 43 homers in 566 AB
    1956: 28 homers in 400 AB

Now, pick your favorite classic or current hitter and see if you can figure out his or her home run percentage in different years of his or her career.

This jail term did not stop Curley from running for Congress and winning in 1910. He ran for mayor of Boston three years later and won, resigning from Congress in 1914 so he could take office. He served as mayor until 1918 and was not reelected, but ran again and won another term in 1922.

Curley was a gifted speaker and was unafraid to insult his rivals. When some of his opponent's supporters showed up at one of his rallies and heckled him, he called them "nothing but a pack of second-story workers, milk-bottle robbers, and doormat thieves" and invited them to come up and see what would happen. Nobody stepped forward.

When in 1913, the Democratic City Committee endorsed his opponent, Curley called the committee "empty egg shells." His biggest political rival was John F. Fitzgerald, who beat him for mayor in 1918.

He ran unsuccessfully for governor of Massachusetts in 1924 and was not reelected as mayor in 1926, but won another mayoral term in 1930. After his term ended in 1934, he ran successfully for governor and served two years, from 1935 to 1937. He ran again for mayor of Boston in 1937 but lost, and ran again in 1941 and lost again. In 1942, he was elected to Congress again and served two terms. In 1945, he was elected mayor of Boston and served in both roles simultaneously. His time as congressman was up in 1947, the same year that he was sentenced to prison for mail fraud. President Harry Truman commuted his sentence and pardoned him for both convictions in 1950, the year Curley's time as mayor ended. By now 75 years old, Curley was not done yet. He ran again, unsuccessfully, for mayor of Boston in 1951 and 1955. He died in 1958.

The Great Depression and World War II

Boston's population soared after the 1929 US stock market crash, with many coming to Massachusetts's biggest city in search of work. The city's Italian and the Irish communities were among the most affected by the Great Depression. While unemployment in Boston as a whole reached about 20 percent, it soared above that for the Irish and Italians. Boston's three Depression-era

(right) James Curley.

(below) A CURLEY FOR MAYOR campaign design in the shape of a Boston subway token, 1929.

mayors were not particularly excited about President Franklin Roosevelt's New Deal policies, and though the federal government forced some policies and agencies upon the city, the New Deal did not change the way Boston politics worked.

As with the rest of America, once the United States entered World War II, employment rates rose dramatically as much of the country was engaged in the production of vehicles, weapons, and supplies for the war effort. One of the hubs for wartime jobs was near Boston, at the Watertown Arsenal, which had existed since the early 19th century but was expanded dramatically to increase its capacity during World War II. The arsenal produced $30 million worth of equipment in 1942 alone.

Because so many Boston men went off to war, many women worked a number of jobs. Nineteen-year-old Martha Barnum worked a 10-ton crane at the arsenal, where 30 percent of the employees were women. Other local area employers included the Boston Navy Yard and a Boston forging shop that hired women to swing 12-pound sledgehammers. War plants in Massachusetts employed between 100,000 and 500,000 women between 1941 and 1945.

The Kennedy Clan

When Patrick Kennedy and Bridget Murphy sailed from Ireland to Boston in 1849, little could they imagine they would be the founders of one of America's best-known and most beloved political dynasties.

Make a WPA Wish List

During the Great Depression, President Franklin Roosevelt created many agencies as part of his New Deal to help kick-start the economy and get people back to work. One of these agencies was the Works Progress Administration (WPA), which was tasked with fixing up America's public works. It gave millions of people—everyone from craftsmen and painters to bricklayers and writers—work during the 1930s.

Many buildings, roadways, and bridges in Boston were fixed or built by WPA workers, from the Boylston Street Bridge over the Boston & Albany Railroad to the Charles Innes Underpass carrying Huntington Avenue under Massachusetts Avenue, the Charlesbank Beach, and the Fort Hill Square Fire Station. The WPA even worked on the Huntington Avenue subway extension, which is now part of the Green Line. Over 1,000 people were employed in this project.

Imagine you are asked to present a list of possible WPA projects to the federal government during the Depression. Which 10 public buildings or roadways in your town or area are in the most urgent need of repairs? Take a walking or driving tour of the area and note which structures are damaged. Make a list of each structure's name, location, and repairs needed. You can enhance the list with photographs. You might even submit this list to your local mayor or town council for their consideration for future funding!

Joseph Kennedy in 1934.

years later he led the Maritime Commission, and in 1937 President Franklin Roosevelt appointed him as ambassador to Great Britain.

Joseph Kennedy's children would be destined for even greater success. John Fitzgerald Kennedy would be president, Robert Francis Kennedy would be a US senator, and Edward "Ted" Kennedy went on to be the third-longest-serving senator in American history, serving nearly 47 years. The Kennedy daughters also made their mark— Eunice founded the Special Olympics, and Jean became ambassador to Ireland. The family has had its share of tragedy. President John F. Kennedy and his brother Robert were both assassinated, their brother Joseph died in a plane explosion during World War II, and their sister Kathleen died in an airplane crash over France. John's son John Jr. also died in a plane crash.

Many of the next generations of Kennedys are also politicians and diplomats, including Patrick (Ted's son, a US Congressman) and Caroline Kennedy (John's daughter, the former US ambassador to Japan).

While the family spread from its Boston roots over the years, Massachusetts is still their sentimental home. The Kennedys have had a three-building compound, where they held family gatherings, at Hyannis Port on Cape Cod since 1926.

The Blizzard of '78

Weather predictions are not always accurate. They sure weren't one winter day in Boston in January 1978, when what was forecasted to be rain wound

The Kennedy name first rose to prominence with the couple's son, Patrick Joseph Kennedy, a successful Boston businessman who served several terms in the Massachusetts House of Representatives. His son, Joseph Patrick Kennedy, was born in 1888 in East Boston. After graduating from Harvard, Joseph married Rose Fitzgerald, daughter of Boston's mayor. Joseph Kennedy was a successful businessman but like his father also aspired to politics. After Franklin Roosevelt was elected president in 1932, Kennedy was appointed as head of the Securities and Exchange Commission. A few up becoming a major snowstorm that dumped 22 inches of the white stuff on the city. Bostonians shook their heads at how inaccurate the weather reports were.

When a new weather system was on its way to New England a couple weeks later, the residents of Boston were not sure what to believe. Nobody panicked, because although some snow was predicted, few people had faith in the weather reports, especially after what had just happened. When snow began to fall the morning of February 6, 1978, people went to work and business went on as usual.

Except it kept snowing. And snowing, and snowing. By early afternoon, the snow was falling at two inches per hour, and workers were planning their early escapes to get home before it was too late. But it was already too late. The roads were clogged with both cars and snow, a dangerous combination. Accidents didn't help matters. Traffic crawled, and the snow continued to fall. Thousands of cars were stranded on Boston-area highways as the snow piled up rapidly, making roads impassable. Many people abandoned their cars and sought shelter.

It was a snowstorm of epic proportions, with 27 inches falling in Boston by the time the storm was over 33 hours later, including a 24-hour record of 24 inches of snow. Sustained winds of more than 35 miles per hour blew for several hours during the peak of the storm, with gusts of 55 to 80 miles per hour. Dozens of people in Massachusetts died during the storm.

Just north of Boston, much of the city of Revere was underwater due to flooding. It took days for

BEANTOWN

Many cities have fun and interesting nicknames that go back decades or even centuries. New York is the Big Apple. Chicago is the Windy City. And Boston? Beantown!

The origin of the nickname is simple: Boston is known for its baked beans, which had been introduced to the earliest settlers in Massachusetts by the local Native Americans. In the 18th century, the settlers began to add molasses to their beans, creating the traditional Boston baked beans that we know today. In use since at least the 19th century, the moniker Beantown (or Bean Town) has been especially popular in the sports pages of newspapers.

When the Boston Braves won the World Series over the Philadelphia Athletics in 1914, the newspaper headlines read, JOY IN BEANTOWN OVER VICTORY. In fact, Boston's National League team was known as the Beaneaters between 1883 and 1906.

Boston in 1964.

The snowstorm of 1978.

Bostonians to dig out of the mess that was complicated by massive snow drifts and leftover snow from the previous storm. One of the notable storm-related losses in Boston was the *Peter Stuyvesant*, a historic 1927 cruise ship turned restaurant, which sank off Pier 4 due to wind and rising waters. All told, the storm caused more than $500 million in damage in New England.

Two Governors, Two Nominees

In 1988, President Ronald Reagan's second term was ending and his two-time vice president,

George Bush, was poised to become the Republican Party's nominee for president, handily beating his main rival, Bob Dole. On the Democratic side, the field was crowded with several candidates, including civil rights leader Jesse Jackson, Congressman Richard Gephardt, former Arizona governor Bruce Babbitt, Senator Paul Simon, and Massachusetts governor Michael Dukakis (who was governor 1975–1979 and again 1983–1991).

It was Dukakis, who had served four terms in the Massachusetts House of Representatives before becoming governor, who wound up with the nomination. A native of the Boston suburb of

Brookline, Dukakis went on to run against Bush in an election campaign where he was portrayed by the Republicans as being too liberal. One campaign issue that sunk Dukakis's chances was his support for a prison furlough program that resulted in the release of a convicted murderer named Willie Horton, who went on to assault someone while on furlough. Another was his opposition to the death penalty. Dukakis lost the 1988 election to Bush 426–111 electoral votes (he won just 9 states) and 53 percent to 46 percent in the popular vote.

The year 2012 was former Massachusetts governor Mitt Romney's time in the presidential election spotlight. Romney, a Utah native who served as governor of Massachusetts from 2003 to 2007, handily beat out three other candidates for the nomination and went on to face popular president Barack Obama in the 2012 general election. The result was a second term for Obama and a second loss for a Massachusetts governor running for president.

In 2016, former Massachusetts governor William Weld (1991–1997) was the vice presidential candidate for the Libertarian Party, which won 3 percent of the popular vote.

The Boston Central Artery

When Interstate 93 (also known as the Central Artery) was built as a partly elevated highway through downtown Boston in the 1950s, many residents complained that it was not only ugly but also cut through and divided neighborhoods. In fact, the new highway displaced 20,000 Bostonians from their homes. Designed to be an efficient passage through the city, when it opened it carried 75,000 vehicles per day. But 30 years later, 200,000 vehicles per day turned I-93 from a highway into a notoriously congested parking lot. Something had to be done. But what?

The ambitious and ingenious solution was to build an 8- to 10-lane tunnel to replace the deteriorating 6-lane elevated highway. Planning started in 1982, and construction began in 1991 on this project, known as the Big Dig. Requiring 15 years to build and 5,000 workers during its peak, it has been compared to some of the largest public works projects in modern history, such as the Panama Canal and the English Channel Chunnel.

BOSTON'S ISLANDS

The harbor at Boston is strewn with islands and large rocks—dozens of them! These little specks of land, ranging between about 2 and 12 miles from Boston's main wharf, were given interesting names, including Bumkin Island, Button Island, Castle Island, Deer Island, Egg Rock, Grape Island, Half Moon Island, Hangman's Island, Hog Island, Little Hog Island, Moon Island, Nut Island, Raccoon Island, Ragged Island, Sheep Island, Snake Island, Spectacle Island, and Sunken Island. There is also Noddle's Island, which in the 17th century was occupied by Samuel Maverick, who built a fort mounted with four cannons; Lighthouse Island (or Beacon Island), which had a lighthouse as early as 1715; and Rainsford Island, upon which a hospital was erected in the 19th century to quarantine those with contagious diseases.

BOSTON SUBURBS

There are many towns surrounding Boston, most of which have long histories of their own. With the advent of the automobile, highways, and the Boston subway system in the 20th century, these towns quickly became suburbs.

Places such as Somerville, Brookline, Newton, Waltham, Arlington, Milton, Needham, and Quincy are now within a half hour's commute of downtown Boston. While considered part of the greater metropolitan Boston area, today these towns still maintain their own identities. Brookline, first settled in 1630, was actually considered part of Boston until it incorporated in 1705. Somerville was also settled in 1630, when John Woolrich came from the Charlestown peninsula "by reason of his trade with the Indians" and built a house there. The farming community of Needham was first settled in the 1640s and incorporated in 1711. The city of Newton, first settled in the 17th century, was originally made up of several settlements whose names are still neighborhoods today: Newton Centre, Newton Highlands, and Newton Upper Falls.

Interstate 93 cut right through the heart of Boston.

In addition to much-improved traffic conditions (it now takes 3 minutes to get through downtown Boston, instead of 20 minutes), one of the other main benefits of the Central Artery tunnel project is the open space where the elevated highway had once been. More than 45 parks and public plazas were created as a result of the Big Dig, and long-severed connections between neighborhoods were restored.

There were other benefits, too. The 12.2 million cubic meters of dirt excavated to create the tunnel was used to cap landfills around New England. Because traffic moves much more smoothly than it used to, carbon monoxide emissions in Boston are down 12 percent from their former levels. The project, which cost more than $14 billion, also extended Interstate 90 through South Boston to Boston Logan International Airport.

The Boston Marathon Bombings

The annual marathon in Boston, held every year on Patriots' Day, is the oldest annual marathon in the world. Started in 1897, the 26.2-mile race has long been a popular event with both runners and spectators. The first race was held the year after the 1896 Olympics, inspired by a marathon that was a prominent part of that competition. It was originally for men only; women were first officially allowed to run the Boston Marathon in 1972, though a few had snuck in and managed to participate before then.

What had always been a joyous and exciting event turned tragic on April 15, 2013, when two

Make a Cut-and-Cover Tunnel

There are a few different ways to create tunnels. In places that require deep tunnels or where the tunnel must be dug through rock, tunnel-boring machines are used to burrow horizontally through the ground.

Another option is the cut-and-cover method, which involves digging a trench, creating a tunnel, and covering up the rest of the trench again. Boston's most ambitious tunneling project was the Central Artery, known as the Big Dig. The project spanned 7.8 miles of highway, 161 lanes miles in all, about half in tunnels. All told, the Central Artery/Tunnel Project (CA/T) placed 3.8 million cubic yards of concrete—the equivalent of 2,350 acres, one foot thick—and excavated more than 16 million cubic yards of soil.

The CA/T created more than 45 parks and major public plazas. What is the ideal shape for a highway or subway tunnel? In this activity, you will create a cut-and-cover tunnel of your own and figure out the answer.

YOU'LL NEED

★ Paper towel tube

★ 8-by-14-inch cardboard of similar thickness to the tube

★ Electrical tape

★ Trowel

You'll test cardboard tunnels of two different shapes, circular and square. For the circular tunnel, simply use the tube from the center of a paper towel roll. For the square tunnel, fold the long side of a piece of 8-by-4-inch cardboard in half, and then fold it in half again. Unfold and bend the edges together to create a rectangular tube. Secure the edges with a long piece of electrical tape along the full length of the tube.

On a sandy beach or in your yard, use the trowel to dig two parallel trenches slightly longer than the length of the tubes, about 1 foot apart and 6 inches deep. Lay each of the tubes into a trench and then cover them both with about 3 inches of sand or dirt. Press down lightly on the soil or sand to make sure it is compacted. Now walk back and forth a few times on top of your covered trenches. Carefully dig up your tunnels and examine them. Which shape held up better?

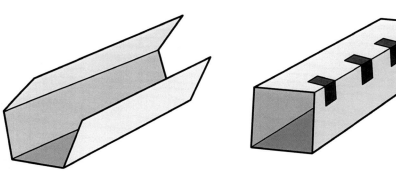

Walking Tour of the Boston Common

The Boston Common is not only a pleasant and historic park to enjoy, it is chock full of historic sites. No trip to Boston is complete without a visit to the Common. If you start from the corner of Boylston and Tremont Streets, the first noteworthy site you'll encounter is the Central Burying Ground. This cemetery was built on former pasture land and was an overflow cemetery for three earlier ones in town. There is a mixture of burials here, including British soldiers who died during the Revolution, American patriot soldiers, foreigners who died while visiting Boston, and notables such as the famed painter Gilbert Stuart. Some of the tombs along the corner of Boylston and Tremont were eliminated for street construction in the 1830s.

Just north of the cemetery is the historic Parkman Bandstand, which dates to 1912. It is the site for concerts and speeches. In 2007, then candidate Barack Obama gave a speech from the bandstand.

Northwest of the bandstand is a placard marking Pope John Paul II's visit to the Common in 1979, where he celebrated his first mass of his landmark trip to the United States.

Head back east from the placard and then north to the Soldiers and Sailors Monument, which dates to 1877 and commemorates Boston's Civil War dead.

From here it is just a hop to the Frog Pond, one of the most beloved family attractions in Boston. Originally a spring-fed watering hole for cattle in the 1600s, a fountain was added by the City of Boston in the 1850s. Though long ago it used to feature frogs, today the pond is better known for its use as an ice skating rink in winter.

If you walk east from the Frog Pond, you will connect with the Freedom Trail. You'll also encounter the Brewer Fountain, a 15,000-pound bronze artwork that dates to 1868.

There is plenty more to see and explore within the Boston Common. You can look online for more information or visit the Visitors' Center within the Common, near the intersection of Tremont and West Streets.

bombs went off 200 yards apart along Boylston Street near the finish line, a few hours after the first racers had crossed. Footage and photos of the chaotic aftermath at the scene quickly appeared on television and in newspapers across the world as word of the horrible attack spread.

The explosions killed three people and injured 264 others, many of them severely. The Red Cross, which had a presence at the race as usual, played a big role in helping victims on the scene and in the days after the bombings, serving 47,000 meals and snacks to those affected.

Law enforcement officials hurried to track down suspects. Four days later, two brothers, natives of the former Soviet republic of Kyrgyzstan, were identified. The city was on lockdown as the suspects tried to escape from the police. In their attempt to flee, they killed a Massachusetts Institute of Technology officer. The older brother, 26-year-old Tamerlan Tsarnaev, was killed in a police shootout, and his 19-year-old younger brother was captured that same day. In 2015, Dzhokhar Tsarnaev was tried and found guilty on 30 counts. He was sentenced to death.

The terror attack jolted the city, which received an outpouring of love from around the world. A two-word motto—BOSTON STRONG—caught on soon after the tragedy and helped unify the city. The Boston Marathon took place as scheduled the next year, with a moment of silence at the beginning of the race in remembrance of those killed and injured in the bombings.

Super!

The Red Sox are not Boston's only professional sports team. Several other highly successful teams have been entertaining fans for many decades.

The Boston Celtics basketball team was founded in 1946 and joined the National Basketball Association (NBA) in 1949. This highly successful team holds the NBA record for most championships won, with 17 victories through 2016.

Another Boston team that has enjoyed success, especially in recent years, is the New England Patriots, a National Football League (NFL) team that won the Super Bowl in 2001, 2003, 2004, 2014, and 2016. Originally formed in 1959 as the Boston Patriots, the team was part of the American Football League until its merger with the NFL in 1970.

The Boston Bruins, founded in 1924 and the country's oldest National Hockey League team, are the city's professional ice hockey team. The team has won six Stanley Cup championships, tied for fourth among all teams for most championships won.

Boston's Future

Boston is a unique city—a thriving modern metropolis that is steeped in America's history. Embracing its past while looking forward, the city continues to be one of the most important in our nation, the capital of New England, and a cradle of democracy.

Boston as seen from the Charles River.

ACKNOWLEDGMENTS

THANKS TO FAMILY AND FRIENDS for their continued support, and thanks to all the folks at Chicago Review Press for continuing to allow me to be a part of this high-quality line of children's books, especially Cynthia Sherry and Jerry Pohlen, with whom I've worked closely for the past 20 years.

RESOURCES

RECOMMENDED FOR FURTHER READING

Eyewitness Travel: Boston. New York: Dorsey Kinderling, 2015.

Hossell, Karen Price. *The Boston Tea Party: Rebellion in the Colonies*. Chicago: Heinemann Library, 2003.

LeVert, Suzanne, and Tamra B. Orr. *Massachusetts*. New York: Marshall Cavendish Benchmark, 2009.

Lukes, Bonnie L. *The Boston Massacre*. San Diego: Lucent Books, 1998.

Panchyk, Richard. *Keys to American History*. Chicago: Chicago Review Press, 2009.

Philbrick, Nathaniel. *Bunker Hill: A City, a Siege, a Revolution*. New York: Viking Penguin, 2013.

Sommer, Shelley. *John F. Kennedy: His Life and Legacy*. New York: HarperCollins Children's Books, 2005.

Stoll, Ira. *Samuel Adams: A Life*. New York: Free Press, 2008.

MUSEUMS

Boston Children's Museum
308 Congress St., Boston, MA 02210
Phone: (617) 426-6500
www.bostonchildrensmuseum.org
Founded in 1913, it is the second-oldest children's museum in the world. It houses more than 50,000 historical and scientific artifacts.

Boston Museum of Science
1 Science Park, Boston, MA 02114
Phone: (617) 723-2500
www.mos.org
With roots going back to 1830, this natural history museum attracts more than 1½ million visitors per year to its 700 interactive exhibits.

Boston Public Garden

4 Charles St., Boston, MA 02116

Phone: (617) 635-4505

www.boston.gov/parks/public-garden

The Boston Public Garden, located in the heart of the city, is one of the most well-known landmarks in Boston. Take a leisurely stroll in the park, as Boston natives and tourists alike have done since the first version of the park was built in 1837.

JFK Presidential Library and Museum

Columbia Point, Boston, MA 02125

Phone: (617) 514-1600

www.jfklibrary.org

The John F. Kennedy Presidential Library and Museum opened in 1979 at its waterfront home on Columbia Point. The museum showcases several permanent exhibits as well as special exhibits.

Massachusetts State House

24 Beacon St., Boston, MA 02133

Phone: (617) 722-2000

www.sec.state.ma.us/trs/trsbok/trstour.htm

The State House is an architectural masterpiece that was designed by famous Boston architect Charles Bulfinch and completed in 1798. It is located on Beacon Hill.

Museum of Fine Arts, Boston

465 Huntington Ave., Boston, MA 02115

Phone: (617) 267-9300

www.mfa.org

Opened in 1876 with 5,600 works of art, this major museum's collection now has 500,000 works of art in a classical building that was built in 1909.

Old State House

206 Washington St., Boston, MA 02109

Phone: (617) 720-1713

www.bostonhistory.org

The Old State House is one of the oldest surviving buildings in Boston. Built in 1713, it was home to the Massachusetts General Court until 1794. The building now serves as a museum.

Paul Revere House

19 N. Square, Boston, MA 02113

Phone: (617) 523-2338

www.paulreverehouse.org

Built in 1680, this building was home to the legendary patriot Paul Revere. It contains period furnishings, including several that belonged to the Revere family.

USS *Constitution* Museum

Building 22, Charlestown Navy Yard, Charlestown, MA 02129

Phone: (617) 426-1812

www.ussconstitutionmuseum.org

Built in 1797 in Boston, the USS Constitution *is the oldest commissioned ship in the US Navy.*

INDEX

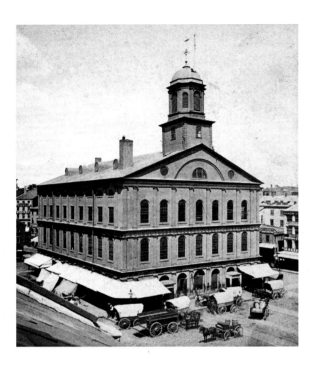

W

978-1-55652-654-1
$16.95 (CAN $19.95)
Also available in e-book formats

Chicago History for Kids
**Triumphs and Tragedies of the Windy City,
Includes 21 Activities**

By Owen Hurd

DESIGNATED A CHICAGO PUBLIC LIBRARY BEST OF THE BEST BOOK FOR 2007

From the Native Americans who lived in the Chicago area for thousands of years, to the first European explorers Marquette and Jolliet, to the 2005 Chicago White Sox World Series win, parents, teachers, and kids will love this comprehensive and exciting history of how Chicago became the third largest city in the U.S. Chicago's spectacular and impressive history comes alive through activities such as building a model of the original Ferris Wheel, taking architectural walking tours of the first skyscrapers and Chicago's oldest landmarks, and making a Chicago-style hotdog. Serving as both a guide to kids and their parents and an engaging tool for teachers, this book details the first Chicagoan Jean Baptiste Point du Sable, the Fort Dearborn Massacre, the Great Chicago Fire of 1871, the building of the world's first skyscraper, and the hosting of two World's Fairs. In addition to uncovering Windy City treasures such as the birth of the vibrant jazz era of Louis Armstrong and the work of Chicago poets, novelists, and songwriters, kids will also learn about Chicago's triumphant and tortured sports history.

978-1-883052-93-5
$17.99 (CAN $23.99)
Also available in e-book formats

New York City History for Kids

From New Amsterdam to the Big Apple, with 21 Activities

By Richard Panchyk

"The main narrative is well stocked with both passages from contemporary documents and photos or other period illustrations."

— *School Library Journal*

It started as New Amsterdam, a tiny 17th-century fur-trading post at the southern tip of Manhattan Island, but it grew to become New York City, a 21st-century metropolis of 8 million people. In this lively 400-year history, children will read about Peter Stuyvesant and the enterprising Dutch colonists, follow the spirited patriots as they rebel against the British during the American Revolution, learn about the crimes of the infamous Tweed Ring, journey through the notorious Five Points slum, and soar to new heights with the Empire State Building and the city's other amazing skyscrapers. Along the way, they'll stop at Central Park, the Brooklyn Bridge, the Statue of Liberty, and many other prominent New York landmarks. *New York City History for Kids* also includes 21 informative and fun activities to better understand the Big Apple's culture, politics, and geography. Kids will build a replica of Fort Amsterdam, paint a Dutch fireplace tile, play a game of stickball, take walking tours of City Hall Park and Fifth Avenue, and more. This valuable resource also includes a time line of significant events and a list of historic sites to visit or explore online.

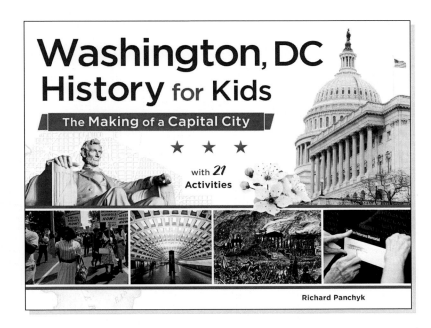

978-1-61373-006-5
$16.99 (CAN $19.99)
Also available in e-book formats

Washington, DC, History for Kids
The Making of a Capital City, with 21 Activities

By Richard Panchyk

"An informational and activity-filled book that will be very useful for late-elementary and middle school history projects."
—*School Library Journal*

In 1790, after seven years of heated debate, the Continental Congress approved a plan to establish the nation's offical capital in a barely populated swamp straddling the Potomac River. Ten years later, in November 1800, Congress gaveled in its first session in the federal city—Washington—in what was then called the Territory of Columbia. *Washington, DC, History for Kids* chronicles the rich and fascinating history of our nation's capital. Its first years were difficult—in 1814 the British invaded and burned the White House, the Treasury Building, and the Half-built Capitol Building—yet the city survived and flourished. During the next two centuries, District residents endured the Civil War at the front lines, witnessed the assassinations of two presidents, erected national monuments, and strove to overcome the city's shameful racial segregation. This lively history also includes a time line, a list of online resources, and 21 engaging hands-on activities. Kids will: gather items for a cornerstone time capsule, take a walking tour of the national mall, research family history through the National Archives, design a memorial for a favorite president, plant a cherry tree, and more.

CHICAGO REVIEW PRESS

Available at your favorite bookstore, by calling (800) 888-4741, or at www.chicagoreviewpress.com